RED
ALERT

Getting in on the Ground Floor: How to Make Money Now—And from Now On—In the New Bull Market
by Stephen Leeb with Donna Leeb

Market Timing for the Nineties: The Five Key Signals for When to Buy, Hold, and Sell
by Stephen Leeb with Roger S. Conrad

The Agile Investor: Profiting from the End of Buy and Hold
by Stephen Leeb and Roger Conrad

Defying the Market: Profiting in the Turbulent Post-Technology Market Boom
by Stephen Leeb and Donna Leeb

The Oil Factor: Protect Yourself and Profit from the Coming Energy Crisis
by Stephen Leeb and Donna Leeb

The Coming Economic Collapse: How You Can Thrive When Oil Costs $200 a Barrel
by Stephen Leeb with Glen Strathy

Game Over: How You Can Prosper in a Shattered Economy
by Stephen Leeb

RED ALERT

How China's Growing Prosperity Threatens the American Way of Life

STEPHEN LEEB with GREGORY DORSEY

BUSINESS
PLUS

NEW YORK   BOSTON

Business Plus
Hachette Book Group
237 Park Avenue
New York, NY 10017

www.HachetteBookGroup.com

Business Plus is an imprint of Grand Central Publishing.
The Business Plus name and logo are trademarks of Hachette Book Group, Inc.

Printed in the United States of America

First Edition: October 2011

10   9   8   7   6   5   4   3   2   1

Library of Congress Cataloging-in-Publication Data
Leeb, Stephen.
    Red alert : how China's growing prosperity threatens the American way of life / Stephen Leeb and Gregory Dorsey. — 1st ed.
        p. cm.
    ISBN 978-0-446-57623-9
    1. China—Economic policy—2000–   2. Energy policy—China.   3. Environmental policy—China.   4. United States—Economic policy—21st century.   5. Energy policy—United States.   6. Environmental policy—United States.   I. Dorsey, Greg.   II. Title.
    HC427.95.L445 2011
    330.973—dc22

                                                                        2011000642

To our children and grandchildren: Tim, Will, Cameron, Bridget, and Erin.

Acknowledgments

As with every book in which I have been an author, my wife, Donna, has played an essential role. In *Red Alert*, Donna made critical contributions to the outline of the book and the structure and content of the preface and first two chapters. Much thanks also goes to Michael and Alexander Poukchanski. Michael has been my chess coach and friend for more than a decade. His insights and deep understanding of chess contributed enormously to my understanding of the limits of computer intelligence and the limits of technology in general. Alexander and Michael are largely responsible for my limited but I think important understanding of Russia. Special thanks go to Patrick DeSouza, whose counsel, both as a colleague and friend, was invaluable. Our thanks to Eveline Chao for her input on daily life in China.

We also want to thank our agent, Al Zuckerman, who was ceaselessly encouraging and insightful about our proposal and many chapters. We are indebted as well to our editor, Rick Wolff, for his guidance and judicious comments, which immensely refined the finished product. We are most appreciative of the efforts of the entire Business Plus team, including Mari Okuda, Roland Ottewell, Meredith Haggerty, and Jen Musico. In addition, Genia Turanova, David Sandell, and Scott Chan, as well as other colleagues at Leeb Group, were a vital source of encouragement and ideas. And thanks to Ray Holland for making what might otherwise be arcane charts infinitely lucid.

Contents

Foreword

The Prussian chancellor Otto von Bismarck once commented sagely that "a statesman is a politician who thinks of his grandchildren." This brilliant nineteenth-century architect of German unification was hardly an unblemished character, but he was an extraordinary strategic thinker and on this point he was right: True national leadership is more than a tactical exercise; it requires a long-term plan. In the West today we have no plan as to how to secure or develop the resources that are the lifeblood of our prosperity, whereas in the East (and particularly China) they do have such a plan. That premise, and the implications that flow from it, are the essence of *Red Alert*.

An avid admirer of Stephen Leeb's work, I believe that the thesis of *Red Alert* must be taken seriously. I have great reason to urge the reader to do so. To my mind, Stephen is one of the greatest long-term strategists of his generation. This is not puffery. Simply put, I have been a beneficiary of his wisdom in ways that have benefited both my mind and my pocketbook: His insights have been a critical component for me in the creation of not merely one, but several successful businesses. His counsel over the years regarding the trajectory of silver, platinum group metals, oil and gas, copper, and the other resources on which I have built my career has, to put it bluntly, helped me make money. In some cases, he has reinforced my own strong convictions, as with hydrocarbons and gold. In others, he has added whole new dimensions to my thinking, such as with copper and, most recently, silver. Stephen's perspectives and knowledge have been incredibly valuable, and I have been privileged to have access to them.

What is extraordinary about Stephen is that, much as I think of him as one of my secret weapons, he's not at all secretive. He publishes an excellent newsletter. He appears regularly on television and at investor conferences. And he has in this book withheld nothing from the public that he has confided to me privately.

The Asian growth story is one to which Stephen was an early subscriber, coining the term "Chindia" long before many of his peers had gleaned the impact of China and India on commodities. Building on this theme, *Red Alert* raises new questions. One does not have to look for phantoms to conclude that the Chinese in particular "get" where the world is going and that, despite remarkable political challenges (including their rural/urban divide and what will be a fraught navigation toward a more sustainable political equilibrium), as well as physical constraints that may yet derail their ambitions (including a shortage of water and arable land), they're prepared to do whatever it takes to survive in an era defined by a pronounced "scarcity" of great resources.

The Chinese understand all too well what their strategists refer to as the "correlation of forces" (what we commonly term the "balance of power") and would appear to have thought through what they need to do to get to the top—and stay there. As Stephen points out, relentlessly and mercilessly, the intellectual and financial preparedness of the Chinese leadership to focus on the struggle for natural resources is only matched, in lopsided symmetry, by the inability of Western leaders to do the same.

That we have precious few if any statesmen, by a Bismarckian standard, is not merely bad luck but systemic. For we are now ill-prepared for the strategic competition in which we are engaged—and well behind the curve in even identifying the problem. I don't believe our leadership has the slightest inkling of the urgency of most of the themes Stephen elucidates in this text. As such, I fear the future shock to us may be so harsh as to be literally "game over" (to harken back to the title of Stephen's previous book) for the classically optimistic, growth-focused "expanding pie" outlook underpinning the American dream. For an explorationist given to taking risks in pursuit of scarce resources, and hence a perennial optimist, this foreboding is a novel experience. This fear crystallizes the importance and timeliness of *Red Alert*.

Like Stephen, I find it hard to see a way out of our conundrum. Putting aside the almost forty years of on-and-off oil shocks, Americans have had opportunities within the past decade alone to do the right thing and "think of our grandchildren"—and yet we squandered the moments amid bipartisan conflict. The trauma of 9/11, the financial crisis that engendered the American Recovery and Reinvestment Act of 2009 and, I might add, the *Deepwater Horizon* disaster in the Gulf of Mexico, presented turning points where a true leader could have seized the day and summoned the popular imagination in favor of a massive program to invest in alternative energy solutions that would have allowed our civilization to break free of its dependency on foreign oil, create new industries, and improve the environment. Unlike a frog that instinctively knows to leap out of boiling water, even obvious shocks to our economic, political, and physical bodies failed to elicit the appropriate survival reflexes.

Immediately upon finishing reading the final draft of *Red Alert*, I read another book by my friend Jonathan Powell, entitled *The New Machiavelli: How to Wield Power in the Modern World*. It turned out to be a worthy codicil to Stephen's work. Of the many brilliant quotes from Machiavelli's writing, one passage stood out as emblematic of our predicament:

> The Romans did as all wise rulers should, who have to consider not only present difficulties but also future, against which they must use all diligence to provide; for these, if they be foreseen while yet remote, admit of easy remedy, but if their approach be awaited, are already past cure, the disorder having become hopeless; realizing what the physicians tell us of hectic fever, that in its beginning it is easy to cure, but hard to recognize; whereas, after a time, not having detected and treated at first, it becomes easy to recognize but impossible to cure.

By the standards of Confucius ("a man who has committed a mistake and doesn't correct it is committing another mistake"), the West's leaders are a woeful lot. The only tender mercy is that their folly is an open book, allowing individuals the ability to prepare for the future.

As befitting a closed regime, hard evidence as to China's true intent is hard to discern. Even a number of Stephen's reference points are but anecdotal. In many respects, of course, it is this connecting of the dots into such a compelling picture that brightly illuminates the dramatic contribution Stephen has made to our understanding of one of the most important stories of our generation.

One does not have to condone China's totalitarian political system or pragmatic opportunism to see that it didn't create the world's resource scarcity. Root causes include underexploration by Western companies decimated by a multidecade bear market in commodities and the lassitude of a political class that chose complacency over farsightedness as soon as oil shocks faded. Blaming China is thus like blaming the fellow who finally arrives to the party and finds that the tastiest morsels have already been consumed from the buffet. Having been encouraged to join the global economy and enjoy prosperity, China feels as entitled to secure the raw materials that are the prerequisites for growth as everyone else. That it is doing so through mercantilist practice rather than the outright colonialism that characterized previous resource imperialism (by the West and Japan) is to its credit.

It is not inevitable that America and China must come to blows. Nightmarish images of our fleets being obliterated by Chinese missiles could be better replaced in the mind's eye with joint patrols by our navies securing trade routes and freedom of navigation. Indeed, the sooner we expunge the concept of China as an "enemy" the better. One doesn't need to be either defeatist or utopian to grasp the reality that, barring a great depression that cleans the slate of global economic competition for the foreseeable future and sets back the global economy (especially China and India), interdependence must of necessity mean collaboration. Let enmity therefore not be a foregone conclusion. As Viscount Palmerston put it so aptly in a March 1, 1848, House of Commons speech, with reference to his own government:

> It is a narrow policy to suppose that this country or that is to be marked out as the eternal ally or the perpetual enemy of England. We have no eternal allies and no perpetual enemies—our interests are eternal and those interests it is our duty to follow.

China may yet become our enemy if we leave each other with no other option—but for now the word "competitor" should suffice, and "collaborator" would be optimal. Of course, by the time we awaken from our slumber, the opportunity to collaborate may be gone and our national interests may well render China a formidable adversary.

When the history of our time has been written, there is a very real possibility that *Red Alert* will be seen to have fallen more into the realm of prophecy than financial advice. Certainly from my experience with Stephen's forecasts, this is more likely than not. Whether people will believe Stephen now more than on previous occasions remains to be seen. Seeing how few of us are plugged in to his outlook, I wonder whether it will take resource shortages and social unrest for us to "get religion." Put another way, we may need blackouts to see the light. I would therefore caution readers to dismiss Stephen's warnings only at their peril.

Thomas Kaplan
Chairman, Tigris Financial Group

Preface

When history books and economic texts are written years from now, the acknowledged root causes of the devastating recession of 2008–09 will be elements that virtually no one considers today. They will also be recognized as having taken a severe toll on the American economy in the decade leading up to the recession. And today they are in the process of radically altering the way our world will look in a few short years.

It's widely agreed that the 2008 recession was the worst financial catastrophe since the Great Depression, the closest the U.S. economy has come in modern times to disintegrating. We have no dispute whatsoever with that judgment. After all, the S&P 500 dropped more than 55 percent from its peak in late 2007 to its bottom in early 2009—the biggest decline since the 1930s.

All major banks were on the dole, as the government handed out nearly a trillion dollars to help keep the financial system from imploding. Two of our three auto companies—American icons—went bankrupt, remaining in existence only through taxpayer-funded bailouts. Home foreclosures hit record levels, while median incomes dropped 4 percent, the greatest yearly drop since the Depression. Unemployment soared.

In a desperate, if belated response, the Federal Reserve pushed short-term interest rates down to zero for an extended period—and even more shocking, it added an additional trillion dollars to the banking system. The monetary base, the most fundamental measure of money in circulation, more than doubled in less than a year. Prior to 2008–09 the sharpest annual gain in the monetary base had been about 35 percent.

————

The depth of the downturn is acknowledged, yet there is massive misunderstanding as to its underlying causes. As a result, there is utter myopia on the part of economists, analysts, government officials, and the public alike over what comes next. There will be no "return to business as usual," for everything we've experienced to date is just a portent of what lies ahead—unless we act promptly, courageously, and intelligently, ignoring the peripheral and concentrating on the real threats. This book endeavors to explain what this means for you. Two words sum up the crux of our thinking:

Commodities and China.

Wait a minute, we can hear you interject. Why are you bringing in commodities and China, of all things, to explain the recent crisis? Isn't it known that the financial catastrophe resulted from a lethal combination of high debt levels—on everyone's part, from consumers to banks to government—and lax regulation? And doesn't this mean that lowering debt and enacting legislation to better supervise banks and other financial institutions and protect consumers will have a good chance of inoculating us against a recurrence?

Yes and no. High debt and a lack of oversight were the immediate catalysts for the debacle. Banks had too much debt, and consumers too had racked up historic amounts of it. And then of course there was Wall Street, which was leveraged to the hilt in its pursuit of profits via arcane debt instruments.

As for regulation, clearly Wall Street had been allowed to run amok. Even former Fed chairman Alan Greenspan, acolyte of Ayn Rand, conceded that the financial crisis had forced him to alter his belief of more than sixty years that the less regulation the better.

Thus in the aftermath of the crisis we are gaining legislation that aims to better protect consumers from unscrupulous lenders and to regulate Wall Street more closely. We also have a mindset that is, at least temporarily, more resistant to debt.

These are perfectly fine developments in their own right. But they do nothing to prevent the events of 2008 from happening again. The reality is that we remain on a path that virtually ensures, if not another full-scale financial debacle, at the least a protracted decline in Americans' economic well-being and lifestyle. It will take a clear understanding and warlike effort to get us off that path and onto one that offers hope of a more vibrant economic future.

———

So let's return to those two words, China and commodities.

To understand why they're so critical and how they pertain both to the recession of 2008–09 and to any hope of a decent economic future, we need to backtrack. One key point to realize is that 2008–09, for all the blinding force with which it hit, didn't mark a sharp, anomalous downturn in the economy. Those end-of-decade years weren't when Americans first started getting slammed. Rather, Americans had been hurting for the entire decade leading up to that catastrophe. Things already had gotten bad, with forces in play that were roiling the economy and playing havoc with the American dream.

Flash back to the beginning of the decade. The tech bubble had burst, tech stocks were crashing, and the economy was just three months short of entering its first recession since mid-1990. When that recession officially began in March 2001, stocks were down more than 20 percent from their highs. Between March 2001 and the terrorist attacks of September 11, stocks fell another 20 percent. After 9/11, policymakers pulled out all the stops, and economic activity bottomed out. The National Bureau of Economic Research declared that the recession had ended in November 2001.

But stocks, in unprecedented fashion, continued to decline and did not start to turn around until March 2003, more than fifteen months after the recession had ended.

Historically, stocks begin to rise in earnest about four to six months before a recession ends. There have been cases where stocks and the economy start to improve together, but never before had there been a fifteen-month lag between a turn in the economy and a new bull market. Not during the Depression, not in the post–Civil War era. This extreme anomaly demands an explanation.

Much of the answer relates to the fact that even as stocks were continuing to decline, a roaring bull market was taking off in another arena: commodities. In the fifteen or so months following the recession's end, copper, for example, gained more than 15 percent. But this was peanuts compared to oil, which gained nearly 100 percent as it soared from the mid-teens to nearly $30 a barrel. Broad-based measures of industrial commodities gained nearly 20 percent, a bull market by any definition. So those looking for a bull market in stocks were just looking in the wrong place.

Throughout the decade, even after the stock market eventually turned up and took off, commodities continued to be the star investments. The S&P 500, from its low in 2003 to its high in 2007, rose more than 85 percent, and more than doubled when you include dividends. In the same period, however, copper rose from about 70 cents a pound to a high of $4, oil climbed more than sixfold from its 2003 low to its 2008 high, and many other industrial commodities made comparable gains.

Understand that what was propelling these gains in commodities was a sharply rising demand from the developing world, and in particular China, whose economy had been growing by about 10 percent a year. China and other developing countries were ravenous for commodities, causing prices to surge. Because those countries were growing so rapidly, they could absorb the rising costs of commodities, as these inputs would generate further growth and profits. For developed countries like the United

States, however, it was a different story: Rising commodity prices, caused by someone else's demand and not our own, caused economic pain.

For the developed world, rising commodities were the worst sort of news, representing a trend that was simultaneously deflationary and inflationary. In 2008 higher commodity prices started to filter through to the inflation numbers. With inflation rising in both the United States and Europe, central bankers began to think about tightening credit. Indeed, the European Central Bank raised interest rates within a month of the collapse of Lehman Brothers, which turned out to be the first domino in the catastrophic chain reaction. The Fed was heatedly considering making the same mistake.

Overlooked was that rising inflation was also a sign that deflationary forces were at work. Yes, higher gasoline prices were inflationary, but they also were a direct hit to consumers' wallets. Economic growth during the 2000s, averaging 1.8 percent, was the slowest since the 1930s, a direct consequence of rising commodity prices.

These GDP numbers, though telling, are an abstraction. The statistic that drives home how bad the decade was is the drop in median family income. In 1999–2000, adjusted for inflation, median family income was roughly $52,000, the highest ever. By 2005 it had fallen to a bit over $50,000, the first multiyear decline since data began being kept in the 1940s. It remained there until 2009, when it dropped to about $48,000.

The decade's decline in median family income, which resulted from an economy that was barely growing as a result of rising commodity prices, would have been bad enough for consumers. But soaring commodities inflict compound damages and they punished consumers in multiple ways. From the middle of the decade to its end, household spending on energy climbed from about 4 percent of typical income to nearly 10 percent. And that was just energy—other commodity price increases added to the cost of housing and food. Soaring commodities amounted to an unprecedented, multifaceted tax on American consumers at a time when those same commodities were holding back economic growth, resulting in a record loss of income!

They also explain the record-high consumer debt levels, which played such a big part in the 2008–09 collapse. Consumers had to borrow hand over fist simply to keep their heads above water.

In 2008, however, as we noted above, the Fed was focused on the inflationary effects of rising commodity prices—in retrospect, clearly the lesser of two economic evils. Six or seven months into a recession, central bankers should have been lowering rates to perk up the economy. With debt levels high, housing prices weak, and powerful deflationary forces at play—that is, sharply rising commodity prices—the decision to ease credit should have been no contest. Yet the Fed, mesmerized by the inflationary threat it saw in rising commodity prices, chose not to loosen, choking off the chance of providing oxygen to a gasping economy.

Any way you look at it, then, rising commodity prices were the essential cause of the Great Recession. They lay behind the decade's sluggish growth, declining income, and high debt levels, and they were responsible for the Fed's decision not to loosen credit in the middle of a recession, which made matters even worse. And lying behind rising commodities was that giant global economic phenomenon, China.

———

Don't get us wrong. We have no interest in painting China as evil or our mortal enemy. China isn't motivated by a desire to destroy us; rather, it's out to improve its own standard of living, a laudable goal for any government. There's no point in demonizing China for pursuing its own economic interests. But as a disciplined, fast-growing economic juggernaut, China poses a massive challenge to the United States and represents a major threat to our economic well-being. And we have only a limited window of time in which to respond to this challenge in any meaningful way.

It's still all about commodities, but the stakes are getting higher than ever, because commodities are becoming scarce. And as we'll show in this book, without securing massive amounts of an extensive array of commodities, our civilization will have little chance of surviving. It will literally run out of energy, which depends on access to a wide range of other commodities. China understands this and is operating accordingly, starting to accumulate commodities of all sorts. Right now, despite the pain of the 2000s, the United States appears not to have a clue.

We find it ironic that if you had to date the beginning of China's huge impact on commodities, it would be close to September 11, 2001. On that day and on all days thereafter, we have been fighting the wrong battles, in the wrong places.

And while we aren't demonizing China, we think it's appropriate to formulate the challenge it poses in terms of an economic war, because the effort needed to maintain our way of life, and all that goes with it, will require a warlike commitment in terms of focus and money. We need to view it as a life-or-death struggle—a struggle to secure the resources that will enable us to switch to an economy built around renewable energies, the only thing that can sustain us in coming decades and beyond.

Right now, it's a war we aren't likely to win, because Americans don't even know we should be fighting it. But we hope this book will help change that. The past decade illuminates the consequences of losing this war. But if we can marshal our minds and our will in the right direction, we believe there's still hope of altering our future toward a brighter path.

———

We hesitate to make predictions or offer a timeline as to how and how quickly events will play out; there are just too many factors at work that could affect how differently our world will look ten or twenty years from now. Yet we can say with high confidence that without the introduction of some unforeseen breakthrough technology, America is inescapably headed for trouble that will make all previous difficult times we've experienced to date look like a walk in the park. Unfortunately, we know of no viable techno-fix candidates that will save the day.

In the meantime, if China's growth continues unabated, the exponential nature of its consumption of finite natural resources will bring about an alarming deterioration in America's material well-being through soaring costs for everything we consume. This is likely to occur even if America gets on the stick and starts to build out its alternative energy production capacity in earnest, committing trillions of dollars to the effort and with the urgency of combating a world war.

If we continue on our present course, doing little to address the issues at hand, we can expect severe dislocations and an irreparable drop in our national income—our children will experience a decidedly lower standard of living.

We will enter a period of prolonged economic contraction. The forced era of unusually sharp frugality due to the soaring cost of living will lead to a dramatically shrinking service sector (currently 70 percent of the economy), chronic high structural unemployment, and the potential for much higher crime rates as desperate people are forced to resort to desperate measures to make ends meet. Fewer people will be able to afford the cost of a college education.

Resource scarcity will also change our physical landscape. We will be driving smaller cars and traveling less due to soaring fuel costs. We will live in smaller houses, and there may well be a mass exodus from the exurbs and suburbs to cities where affordable public transportation is available.

In a worst-case scenario, resource scarcity could bring about global resource wars, as the fight for critical materials currently believed to exist in abundance (copper, silver, and zinc, for instance) moves from boardrooms where corporate takeovers are now conducted to the field where soldiers, sailors, and airmen vie to secure must-have resources by other means.

Here at home, the hardships that develop as a consequence of resource shortages could potentially be a catalyst for a massive change in how America is governed. As with the socialist and fascist movements that gained momentum during the Great Depression, the difficult era we've embarked upon will engender more extreme political views that could ultimately lead to a more autocratic form of government.

In short, everything we hold dear that is the American way of life is at risk.

Keep in mind that soaring commodity prices threaten to spark a sequence of deep recessions followed by periods of perhaps modest growth that quickly push prices much higher again, repeating the cycle. The contractions will temporarily reduce demand for basic commodities, drawing out the process of resource depletion. But the end results are likely to be no different, with America's stature in the world greatly diminished, our standard of living significantly lower than what we've become accustomed to, and our disposable incomes dramatically curtailed, the aftereffect of the soaring costs of life's necessities and everything else.

RED
ALERT

Chapter 1

The Enlightened Ruler Lays His Plans Well Ahead

The first salvo of a potentially civilization-altering war between China and the United States was recently fired by China—and passed by almost unnoticed. It failed to inspire the galvanizing call to arms needed to unite politicians and the American people and drive us into action. Absent an early morning raid on Pearl Harbor, an attack such as we experienced on 9/11, or the sinking of a *Lusitania*, we carry on as if we have business as usual.

And this time the shot across the bow came quietly, without drama, in the form of a matter-of-fact utterance of the word "no" spoken across a conference table. The time was December 2009 and the place was Copenhagen, at a much-anticipated conference of delegates from 193 nations, gathered to try to devise a coordinated framework to combat global warming.

Hopes had been running high that an internationally binding

agreement could be reached that would satisfy both the United States and China, the two nations whose acceptance was essential for a workable accord. And initially China seemed ready to deal. The general assumption was that the Chinese were finally feeling pressure from the West.

Spurring this optimism was that several weeks before the gathering, the Chinese—widely viewed as the world's greatest contributor to global warming—had announced extremely ambitious plans to curb CO_2 emissions. Most striking was its plan to generate 15 to 20 percent of its primary energy consumption from alternative energies—wind, solar, hydro, and nuclear—by 2020.

But even as China was winning praise from environmentalists for these plans, its actions at Copenhagen were anything but conducive to a new agreement that would genuinely confront climate change. The conference ended in disappointment, with a watered-down agreement and without hard-and-fast targets for reducing carbon emissions. At China's insistence, even language that called for rich countries to set a target to cut their emissions by 2050 (without a quid pro quo from developing countries) was omitted from the final document. President Obama returned to Washington essentially empty-handed. With no concrete treaty to point to, the United States and other developed nations had no incentive to act unilaterally. Instead, they would largely leave carbon reduction to the free market. From almost everyone's point of view, the conference had been a dismal failure.

One winner, however, did emerge from the Copenhagen talks: China. In what one day will be recognized as a brilliant sleight of hand, China managed to simultaneously quash any global effort to deal with climate change, to keep itself free to continue to emit carbon as needed to promote its own growth, and yet still to win plaudits for its seeming newfound commitment to pursuing renewable energy within its own borders.

If there seems some illogic there, from China's perspective it all makes perfect sense. For by warding off meaningful action by others, China positioned itself to ensure its own energy future. The Chinese have done this by cornering the market on a host of increasingly scarce natural resources vital to building its alternative energy infrastructure (and indeed necessary for other infrastructure projects that are key to China's other main goal, bringing its masses of peasants into the modern world). These natural resources are finite and growing scarcer. There aren't enough of them to go around—and the more the world turns to alternative energies, the faster they will be depleted. As China amasses these dwindling resources, other countries, including the United States, will—literally—be left out in the cold.

The modern-day war with China, which has already started, is all about resource scarcity. This phenomenon started a while back with peak oil, the idea that increases in oil production will not be able to keep up with increases in demand—or more specifically that oil production will top out. Peak oil, which used to be a fringe belief, has now gained a greater degree of mainstream acceptance. The International Energy Agency, which represents twenty-eight countries, including the world's largest developed economies, had until recently been a cheerleader for abundant oil. In the

The IEA's Projection of World Oil Production by Type

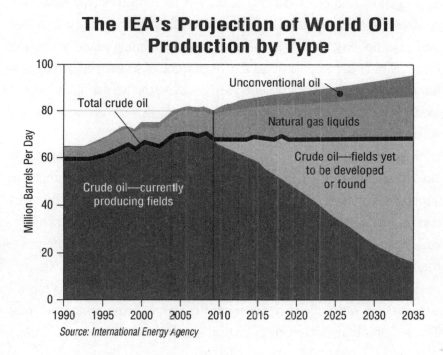

Source: International Energy Agency

middle of the last decade the agency was predicting that conventional oil production would easily top 120 million barrels a day by 2030. By November 2009, however, the IEA had changed its tune and was predicting that conventional oil production would peak by 2020, and a year later it acknowledged that the world reached a peak in conventional oil in 2006.

The organization now believes any increases in oil production after 2020 will only come from nonconventional sources such as tar sands. It is not inconsistent with the IEA prediction to assume that increases in oil production have already reached the point where they will not be able to satisfy increases in demand.

Hidden Ambitions of the Chinese

China's actions at Copenhagen and indeed its development of alternative energy during the past several years suggest the Chinese have realized that a peak in worldwide oil production is imminent—probably within the next decade. And oil is just one of many vital resources that China recognizes are peaking. Coal is another fossil fuel that, contrary to widely held assumptions, will be in short supply in the coming years. No wonder China, which depends on coal for 70 percent of its energy use, is now frantic to develop alternative energies, realizing that to maintain gains in its standard of living it needs to build out a non–fossil fuel energy system with alacrity.

Equally clear is that China realizes that the problem of resource scarcity hardly ends with fuels. Three metals that are critical to completing a wholesale switch to renewable energies—silver, copper, and zinc—are each reaching supply limits, according to academics, leading mining companies, and the U.S. Geological Survey. The implications of shortages in these metals are staggering.

For China to replace a third of its electricity with solar would require almost three times as much silver as is currently being mined per year. This not only makes it unlikely that China can rely on solar energy alone; it

Life of Mine Reserves for Selected Commodities at 2009 Production Levels in China

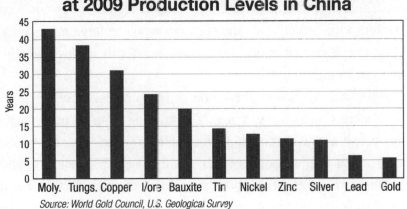

Source: World Gold Council, U.S. Geological Survey

more or less precludes other countries, including the United States, from utilizing solar on a large scale. As for copper, at the current extraction rate we should mine the world's economically viable copper in just thirty years. Factor in the increasing demand to build out the power grid as more and more renewable power generation comes onstream, for hybrid cars, and in emerging economies for better housing, appliances, and other goods, and we could exhaust those deposits even faster.

The logic behind the seeming contradiction between China's actions at Copenhagen and its grand plans to adopt alternative energy technology now should be much clearer. The People's Republic is not building alternative energy because it has suddenly gotten religion on climate change—if that were the case, it would have wanted Copenhagen to result in a treaty binding all participants. Rather, it's moving forward as quickly as it can to obtain essential materials *before* the developed world mobilizes with the same goal. It is rushing forward before large quantities of these indispensable commodities run out. The United States, in contrast, is doing nothing to prepare for the trouble that lies ahead.

A successful outcome of the Copenhagen talks would have sped the worldwide adoption of alternative energy. Were the United States and other developing nations to proceed with a rapid build-out of their own alternative energy infrastructure, the demand for raw materials would skyrocket, prices would soar, and scarcities would emerge more quickly. By short-circuiting that effort, the Chinese bought themselves breathing room to enact their plans.

To give you an idea of the scope of the problem, consider that at today's prices China's avowed goal of converting 15 to 20 percent of its energy consumption to renewables means that over the next ten years its average annual spending on renewables will exceed $350 billion, or about three times what the entire world spent on renewables in 2008. For the Chinese to reach their goal, critical commodities will become so scarce, including those obtainable from recycling, that the rest of the world will have almost no chance of implementing alternative energies on any meaningful scale to catch up, leaving China alone with an effective alternative energy infrastructure.

It's important to realize that the Chinese are relentlessly long-term thinkers. Their leaders don't have to answer to a fickle electorate every two years. They are willing to think in five-, ten-, even twenty-year increments and have proven themselves remarkably good at achieving goals set in past five- and ten-year plans. Indeed, in the alternative energy area, where the country is already the largest producer of solar and wind energy, they have far exceeded past targets. They not only work toward long-term goals, but they are quick to take advantage of others' weakness. Above all, they are motivated by a desire to keep China independent, lest it lose control of its grand destiny.

In discussing its renewable energy plans, China has avoided mentioning peak oil or peak resources, other than in the occasional academic article. Instead, the Chinese government couches its plans under the guise of clean energy. Thus, China presents its plans under the pretext of controlling greenhouse emissions and pollution, so its accumulation of resources is being met with ready acceptance by the world community, where environmental concerns are becoming widely accepted and the necessity for clean, renewable energies almost a religion. At the same time, if the earth does warm, the Chinese will gain more than other countries, which, since they produce a much smaller portion of their energy needs from clean sources, will have to cut back their standards of living more sharply.

China's pursuit of these goals will have major economic repercussions on the rest of the world. Prices for commodities, which as a group increased by as much as 80 percent last decade, depending on the index you use—largely as a result of Chinese demand—will keep rising, perhaps prohibitively so. Americans will not just be paying $10 or more for a gallon of gasoline, everything we buy—food, clothing, electronics, you name it—will cost much, much more. We could also be faced with a prolonged contraction in our economy, with declining real (inflation-adjusted) incomes and double-digit unemployment the norm.

As this book goes to press, some analysts have argued that China is overspending on its infrastructure, that the country has too much industrial capacity and has built too many railroads, too many roads, too many office buildings, and too many homes. To which we say in a loose translation of an old Chinese proverb, "Wait and see."

Their infrastructure spending is akin to a farmer who knows fertilizer prices are going to soar indefinitely. Rather than buying only what he needs for today, the farmer is likely to buy and store as much fertilizer as he can now, rather than potentially having to pay much more for decreasing quantities of this crucial input later on and risking a declining harvest in the process. The so-called bubbles so many have pointed to as inherent in recent Chinese investments are a significant down payment on their long-term plan.

Let us try and put this in a cultural perspective: A highly successful friend with a long career of doing business in China noted psychological experiments that compare the neurological response of Westerners and Easterners to viewing pictures. The results show that people in the West are almost totally focused on a picture's center, where the action lies. Easterners tend to focus on the picture as a whole—to understand the context and, by extension, the reasons behind the action.

The Wrong Priorities

Unlike China, our dysfunctional government is so divided by partisan politics that it can't find common ground on a wide array of highly important issues, such as health care or tort reform. It has, however, found time for wasteful pork spending unrelated to the bills to which it was attached (more than nine thousand earmarks worth $16.5 billion in 2010 alone), or squandering time and effort on the trivial, such as legislating a college football national championship playoff system. Our political and economic systems don't lend themselves to tackling major problems until they reach crisis proportions.

We're concentrating today on clearly visible threats, those right in front of our noses: Iraq, Iran, Pakistan, North Korea, and others that we address in a rather straightforward manner with diplomacy and force. But we're missing the surrounding, yet critical problem of resource scarcity, which will affect us for generations to come. The Chinese, on the other hand, are seeing the bigger picture. They're seizing on the environmental movement as a pretext to accumulate massive amounts of essential resources— copper, zinc, silver, to name a few—to attempt to gain an insurmountable lead in dealing with the urgent problem of impending resource scarcity.

Moreover, not only do the Chinese political and economic systems lend themselves to recognizing and addressing the central problems facing the world in the twenty-first century, but China's leadership is largely comprised of men with backgrounds in the hard sciences. Premier Wen Jiabao, for instance, is a geologist, while Hu Jintao, the country's Paramount Leader, holds a degree in hydraulic engineering from Tsinghua University, the nation's top-ranked school. Xi Jinping, Hu's presumptive successor, holds a degree in chemical engineering. In the United States, on the other hand, the vast majority of top government officials are lawyers by training, predisposed to look no farther ahead than the next election.

What's more, China, with its rapidly growing economy, a domestic market hungering for consumer goods, a huge trade surplus, $3 trillion in foreign currency reserves. and modest external debt, is in far better financial shape to surmount this grim scenario than the United States with its $14 trillion (and climbing) federal debt burden and anemic economy.

China's leaders are following a strategy prescribed twenty-six centuries ago by Sun Tzu, the revered general and philosopher who said, "The enlightened ruler lays his plans well ahead; the good general cultivates his resources." It has launched a challenge that should be treated as nothing less than a war. Copenhagen should serve as a clarion call for the West: If we are to have any chance of meeting China head-on we need to respond in kind—recognizing we'll need to commit far more money and effort than we've put into any conventional war we've ever fought. But first we need to realize how high the stakes really are, and there are no signs that as a nation we do.

What kinds of costs are we talking about? Consider the cost of installing 1,000 gigawatts of alternative energy, about enough to meet a quarter of America's current needs. No matter how we slice it, we come up with a figure close to $5 trillion—and that might be conservative in view of the massive expenditures that will have to be made on transmission infrastructure. For perspective, World War II is estimated to have cost between $3 trillion and $4 trillion.

Our need to wean ourselves off imported oil is serious and urgent; we need to stop playing politics and unite under one banner. During World War II, we buckled down and converted factories to munitions production at record speed. We need to develop alternative energy just as quickly now—in far more than just token gestures.

As tragic as the Fukushima Daiichi disaster was, we should not turn our backs on nuclear power. Additionally, we should not allow bureaucratic red tape to throttle the development of essential projects. While safety should be the utmost priority, we need to shorten the time between approval of a new nuclear reactor and its completion. A new offshore wind farm should not face prolonged delays because it may mar the view from a politician's or wealthy constituent's beach house. And we cannot settle for token government funding for energy research when our adversary is spending on an order of a magnitude greater on the same endeavor.

How we respond to this challenge will have a meaningful impact on our future standard of living. If we do what's needed sooner rather than later there's a reasonable chance we can maintain a standard of living similar to what we've become accustomed to. And from crisis comes opportunity. If we act soon and determinedly, the steps we take to surmount this challenge could even prove to be an engine for growth and prosperity. The longer we delay, the more likely we are to surrender our leading position in the world. If we put off preparations too long, our neglect could end up destroying much of what we regard as the American way of life.

Chapter 2

China's Environmental Smokescreen

In the assault it has launched to corner the market on natural resources, China has cleverly and deliberately wrapped itself in the green mantle of environmentalism. But as we indicated in the last chapter, the Chinese haven't suddenly gotten religion on environmentalism—it's essentially a sham. The danger is that while the United States and the rest of the world are viewing China's pursuit of renewable energies in a positive light, as a welcome signal of its eagerness to cut its carbon emissions, we will overlook China's real game plan—which is to gain an insurmountable lead in obtaining the dwindling natural resources essential for alternative energies. If we don't challenge China soon, we will end up being duped out of our civilization and our future. It's that serious.

Willing to Pollute

We realize that people throughout the world who are committed to combating global warming could be offended by our arguments. After all, gaining China, the world's most populous country and main carbon emitter, as an ally in the fight appears to be a major plus. Being told that this supposed ally is a false friend could understandably stir up cries that we're somehow trying to undermine their cause.

So what evidence is there that China's newfound environmental zeal is nothing more than a smokescreen? Item number one is China's mixed attitude when it comes to combating the severe pollution plaguing much of its country.

It's no secret that China is one of the most polluted nations on earth. It loses a million acres of productive land a year because of human activity, abetted by lax regulatory enforcement and a growth-at-any-cost mindset. It opens another coal-fired power plant every few days to power factories that belch out harmful emissions at an unprecedented rate. Its greatest rivers are too polluted to eat fish from or even touch. Surgical masks are essential in many of China's cities, where lung disorders have become endemic.

In one publicized incident, villagers from Hunan province suffering from lead poisoning as a result of exposure to illegal emissions of heavy metals from a nearby manganese smelting plant were traveling by bus for medical care when they were detained by the police on the charge of "disrupting traffic" on the mere suspicion that their intention was to protest environmental conditions. Two were held for six months. The factory owner's history of polluting was well known to the local environmental department. But even after the villagers' plight was documented, authorities remained unapologetic for their arrests.

Prior to the 2008 Summer Olympics in Beijing, the government ordered the temporary shutdown of approximately a quarter of the nation's factories and enforced a strict rationing system to keep millions of cars off the road. The move did the trick, and air quality improved immensely. People commented on the beauty of sunsets, a simple pleasure that had long been absent. But when the last race was run, life returned to normal and the familiar brown smog soon descended over Beijing again.

And perhaps most significant, as was shown on television's *60 Minutes*, China encourages imports of highly toxic electronic waste—old computers, cell phones, and so on—from other nations, including the United States, even though such imports are officially illegal. Chinese children have been filmed playing in such waste. This goes beyond inadequacy at fighting pollution into actually courting it.

China acknowledges that it has a pollution problem. And we have no doubt that, all things being equal, it would love to clean up its act. Still, what's equally clear is that when it comes to pollution, China makes some key trade-offs that belie anything resembling a genuine conversion to environmental purity. The government may indeed be concerned with the impact rising sea levels may have on the country, but that's a ninety- or hundred-year problem, and for now Chinese leaders are more concerned with tackling the more pressing twenty- or thirty-year issue of resource scarcity. When it's a choice between abating pollution and securing natural resources, resources win hands down.

One of the easiest ways to secure those resources is through recycling what has already been mined. Precious metals recycler Umicore estimates that 3 percent of the world's annual gold and silver production and 13 percent of its palladium production is used in mobile phones, laptops, and PCs. Recapturing precious metals in discarded electronics has become big business: Recycling of e-waste is now a $5.7 billion industry globally and is expected to reach $14.6 billion by 2014, according to the consulting firm ABI Research, with China taking in the lion's share. Competition is so stiff among recyclers in China that people are paid for their junk.

China's capital of e-waste recycling, Guiyu, is located in Guangdong province, about four hours' drive from Hong Kong. Prior to 1995, when the town started taking in e-waste, the area was predominantly rice paddies. Today, Guiyu is the country's largest e-waste recycler/dismantler, but there are other towns like it around the country, and more are springing up. Approximately 90 percent of the town's revenue comes from recycling. When you're still twenty minutes away by car you can smell the foul fumes emanating from the town. Yet the Guiyu website proudly boasts that the town makes $75 million a year from the e-waste business.

Guiyu has a permanent population of about 100,000, and another 100,000 migrant workers are employed there. The migrants usually come from places like Sichuan, a poor mountainous area in west-central China. There is now direct bus service between Guiyu and Urumqi in the far west of China that ferries poor, mostly Muslim residents to jobs in the east. Judging by the many BMWs plying the town's roads, plenty of Guiyu locals are prospering from the e-waste business. The migrant laborers, however, aren't so fortunate. Their pay averages around $1.50 per hour (with sixteen-hour days commonplace), which puts owning a shiny new car far out of reach.

The town is primarily made up of two- and three-story buildings/houses in which the ground floor serves as the workspace where all the sorting and dismantling of the e-waste happens. The most toxic activities of the process include heating up circuit boards on giant hot plates or using acid baths to remove the sought-after metals. The work is conducted primitively, often without gloves, respirators, or protective gear of any kind, which exacerbates the danger, on top of the fact that there really is no safe way to dismantle these electronics in the first place. The extracted gold, silver, copper, and other metals are then sold to electronics manufacturers and smelters.

In addition to heavy concentrations of mercury, cadmium, lead, and other metals in the town's soil, the burning of discarded plastic has released dioxins and other hazardous chemicals that have poisoned the environment. Safe drinking water has to be imported from afar. Conditions were so bad in 2005 that when the Shantou Medical School tested Guiyu schoolchildren, they found that more than 80 percent had lead poisoning. Pregnant women in the town suffer from elevated rates of miscarriages, and other abnormal health issues abound. The workers know what they are doing is dangerous to their health, but their feeling is that they are poor and need the money, so they carry on.

In their exposé of Guiyu, the *60 Minutes* news crew used hidden cameras and the Asians in their group were in disguise as peasants.

Nevertheless, as we learned through the head of Greenpeace's toxics campaign in China, who was present during the filming, within minutes of their entering the town everyone knew they were there. The mayor had them picked up to come talk to him and asked them not to film the town. When the crew went to take shots of a river, its banks lined with piles of e-waste, a band of people appeared, including hired thugs hitting the cameras, intent on intimidating the crew.

The *60 Minutes* story along with others like it created a great deal of unwanted publicity for Guiyu. The story became such an embarrassment that China's environmental protection agency paid the town a visit. But the inspection was preannounced and, magically, it didn't find anything amiss. The people running these illegal businesses now lock their workers indoors to hide their activity. So the workers must now contend with all the toxins with little or no ventilation. The *China Daily*, a government mouthpiece, has actually run stories since then claiming that no hazardous activity goes on in Guiyu and that nobody suffers from any health problems.

The central government may be embarrassed by this e-waste recycling, and it certainly has the power to permanently shut down the activity, but the illegal work continues. Why in the world would the Chinese government be willing to permit this, piling on to the country's already massive pollution woes? The answer is that while electronic wastes are devastating to the health of people exposed to them, they also contain significant amounts of metals such as gold, silver, palladium, and copper, nonrenewable resources that are critical in implementing renewable energies.

On another front, though it has drastically curtailed exports of rare earth elements in the past few years, citing concerns about the environment, China has made it clear that it will move ahead with mining its considerable reserves of these minerals. Rare earth minerals are essential to alternative energies, for electric and hybrid cars, wind turbines, solar panels, energy-efficient LED lightbulbs, and many other applications, including night vision gear and range finders used for national defense, and China controls approximately 97 percent of the world market.

Once rare earth–bearing ore is mined by conventional means, it must be processed to separate the respective pure forms of the elements. This is done using acid and solvents that then must be disposed of. In China, the runoff from the wastewater in the mines' tailings ponds—such as fluorine, various acids, and radioactive materials—routinely finds its way into the soil and water table, with devastating consequences to the food chain and human health.

By contrast, while the United States also has abundant reserves, its lone rare earth minerals mine at Mountain Pass, in California's upper Mojave Desert, was shut down in the late 1990s over pollution concerns and is only now resuming commercial operations.

Short-Circuiting Copenhagen

China's behavior at Copenhagen, to which we alluded in chapter 1, is another sign of its lack of genuine environmental zeal. Let's look at this in more detail.

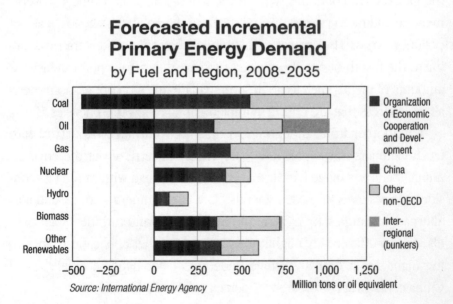

Forecasted Incremental Primary Energy Demand
by Fuel and Region, 2008-2035

Source: International Energy Agency

Shortly before world leaders gathered in Copenhagen in December 2009, China's leadership outlined its long-term plans to curb carbon emissions. It pledged to cut carbon intensity per unit of GDP by 40 to 45 percent by 2020 (compared to 2005 levels). To achieve this, it would seek to generate more than 15 percent of its primary energy consumption from alternative energies—wind, solar, hydro, and nuclear. Such energies currently account for 8 percent of China's total energy usage. And by 2030, its goal was for renewable energies to generate 20 percent of its primary energy consumption. Moreover, the Chinese made it clear that they considered these targets to be conservative. ·

Earlier it had been widely believed that the Chinese would be the biggest obstacle to real progress at Copenhagen. But once they announced these aggressive goals, there was optimism that a deal could be reached, even though clearly it still wasn't going to be easy.

Some of the stumbling blocks were almost laughable. Saudi Arabia, for instance, came to the summit with the position that oil exporters should be compensated for lost revenues if measures were adopted that lowered demand for crude oil—a demand akin to a drug dealer's insisting his addicted customers would have to continue paying him even after emerging from a rehab program having kicked their habit.

China and India, meanwhile, were seeking at least $200 billion a year in aid, starting in 2012, from wealthy countries to developing states, who said they'd reject any accord that didn't include financial aid for their efforts to curb carbon emissions. The United States had offered to help raise $100 billion a year by 2020, but the offer was light on specifics. It was also contingent on verification that emissions actually were being cut, something China would not agree to.

But while all these issues were sticky, there still was room for negotiation and compromise. In the end, however, while Copenhagen did conclude with the first resolution ever in which developing and developed nations alike signed off on the necessity of reaching a climate accord, it failed to result in a binding treaty. The United States left without offering to make any important changes in its environmental policy, and the Chinese stuck only with their initial promise to meet strong renewable energy goals by 2020 and beyond.

The United States and China each accused the other of stonewalling, but published accounts from individuals in the negotiating room indicate it was the Chinese far more than the Americans who stood in the way of a mandatory treaty. Mark Lynas, a British national, sat in as a representative of the Maldives, an island nation in the Indian Ocean that could be threatened with extinction from rising sea levels. Lynas reported in the *Guardian* (and was confirmed by another diplomat in the *Independent*) that China's representative, to everyone's surprise, insisted that targets for industrialized nations—which previously had been agreed upon as an 80 percent cut in emissions by 2050—be removed from the treaty.

This curveball makes no sense if you take the country's newfound stance on climate change at face value. However, in light of China's long-term plans to adopt alternative energy, it makes perfect sense. If the developed nations were, by treaty, committed to reducing greenhouse gas emissions, it would require that they begin building out their alternative energy infrastructure sooner rather than later. For China that would mean fierce competition for the world's dwindling resources.

Most telling, perhaps, was China's behavior on the last day of the conference. Leaders of the major developing and developed countries, including President Obama, had assembled in a final attempt to have the conference produce a meaningful, binding treaty. But one key leader did not show up: Chinese premier Wen. Instead, He Yafei, China's vice foreign minister, took a seat at the table. He is a career diplomat who runs the foreign ministry's North American department; his résumé includes stints at the United Nations and as an arms control negotiator. But he lacked the power of the heads of state sitting around the table: the authority to make real decisions. This calculated move to send He in place of Wen was a diplomatic sleight of the highest order. The clock was ticking for a climate deal, and China's junior representative was unable to speak for his government. He had to leave the room to phone his superiors.

Later, Wen said he didn't attend because the Chinese delegation wasn't actually invited (despite the fact that China's name had been on the invitation). But even after learning the high-level identities of those gathered around the table and of their desire to have China's leader present, Wen chose to stay in his hotel room just a ten-minute drive away.

Later that evening, a last-ditch meeting not on the schedule but arranged by Obama aides took place. It was supposed to be a direct meeting between Obama and Wen but ended up including the leaders of India, Brazil, and South Africa (who, with China, had been acting as a united front at the conference). Premier Wen was hosting the undisclosed meeting of the four developing countries in the same room where he was slated to meet President Obama. The meeting of the four developing countries went on longer than planned. It also surprised the Obama team, who had been informed earlier that the delegates from the other three nations had already left Copenhagen for their respective countries. A U.S. official later characterized the agreement that resulted from this eleventh-hour meeting, which included a means for monitoring each country's greenhouse gas emissions, as an "historical step forward." But that was face-saving spin, as the agreement did nothing to fight climate change.

China's actions at Copenhagen make it plain that it has no interest in really fighting global warming. If it had been sincere in such a goal, it would have wanted a treaty that would bind all nations. Instead, it made sure that no such treaty emerged.

This behavior, while contradictory to China's public stance, was completely consistent with China's view of its own self-interest. Had there been a binding treaty, developed countries, and in particular the United States, would have been farther along the path to taking the next step: voting to take decisive action aimed at reducing their own carbon emissions. But without a treaty that mandated action by all nations, our efforts to curb carbon emissions by the robust development of alternative energies are almost certain to remain patchwork.

And thus China succeeded brilliantly in its true underlying purpose: to be able to continue to rapidly build out its own alternative energy infrastructure, obtaining the necessary resources while they're still available and unhindered by serious competition for them by other nations.

The foot-dragging continued in Bonn, Germany, in April 2010 in the first gathering of climate diplomats after the Copenhagen talks. This time around, China's surrogate, Sudan, managed to convince a handful of nations to join it and Saudi Arabia (which had already made it clear that it was not interested in adopting a climate treaty) in demanding that the nonbinding deal agreed upon in Copenhagen be excluded from future climate talks.

Spearheading the drive was Bernarditas de Castro Muller, a Philippine national and veteran diplomat who had served as her country's lead climate negotiator before being dropped by the Arroyo administration ahead of the Copenhagen talks. She was adopted by Sudan to serve as the coordinator and spokesperson of G77 and China, the main negotiating bloc representing the interests of developing countries.

Muller described Copenhagen as a "trauma," though Sudan has virtually no industry to speak of, does not emit measurable quantities of greenhouse gases, and is not in the vanguard in taking measures to slow global warming. At issue in Bonn was Muller's call for greater "transparency" and "inclusiveness" under United Nations principles that every nation on the planet, regardless of its size and industrial clout, should have a say in the wording of any climate accord.

Subsequent UN global warming discussions have also failed to make progress on greenhouse gas emissions. Yet China has continued to burnish its green image in spite of its own rising CO_2 emissions, all the while berating the United States for not addressing its "historical responsibility" for rising atmospheric CO_2 levels.

Environmental Infighting

Yet another circumstance shows that China has seized upon the environmental cause as cover for pursuing its own unstated agenda of amassing natural resources before anyone else does. It's a striking fact that China jumped aboard the environmental train just when the science of global warming was lurching off the tracks as a result of what the media dubbed "Climategate." Hacked emails from the Climatic Research Unit of the University of East Anglia showed that some environmentalists, though not necessarily wrong about the future, were behaving more as crusaders than as objective scientists. It appeared that some data that might have raised questions about global warming had been selectively withheld or deleted. China could have used these revelations as a way of continuing to balk at the notion that it should cut carbon emissions, arguing that more time was needed to study the underlying science. Instead, China has gone so far as to become one of the main defenders of environmentalists against the withering criticism that Climategate has engendered.

In a February 13, 2010, article in the *Shanghai Daily*, a major Chinese newspaper that's available in English and other languages, a Chinese commentator spoke up for environmentalists who were backpedaling on earlier predictions that the Himalayan glaciers would completely melt by 2035. The attacks by climate change skeptics, the commentator argued, were "designed to bury whatever hopes still exist for signing a successor treaty to the Kyoto Protocol. But how justified are these attacks, particularly the criticism of the Intergovernmental Panel on Climate Change, the United Nations body that has set the gold standard for analyzing global climate change? . . . There is also unholy glee . . . about destroying an icon of the anti–global warming movement." The editorial then went on to offer a powerful defense for the prediction of the disappearance of the Himalayan glaciers by 2035.

In parsing China's new stance on global warming and its befriending of environmentalists, two additional points are relevant. First, as an underpinning for the aggressive pursuit of alternative energies that it has announced, global warming makes a lot more sense than if China had said it was seeking to cut pollution at home. That's because, as we saw above, many of China's ongoing activities ignore the need to cut pollution—so using pollution as a rationale could have raised questions and invited attacks on the grounds of inconsistency.

The second consideration requires a short digression into the nature of today's global environmental movement as it relates to efforts to switch from fossil fuels to renewable energies. There are two main groups pushing today for renewable energies. The first group is the pure environmentalists, who argue that we need renewable energies to reduce global warming and save the planet. Those in the second group, including peak oil adherents, say we need renewable energies because of fast-approaching resource scarcities—we're running out of sufficient levels of usable fossil fuels.

If this might not seem a very important distinction, the fact is that for the most part these groups rarely support one another and indeed are viewed by both the mass media and the academic world as quite distinct.

In Jared Diamond's well-known book *Collapse*, for instance, the entire focus is on how environmental damage destroys civilizations. In discussing modern-day China, his argument centers almost solely on pollution and global warming. Resource depletion is barely mentioned.

In contrast, Joseph Tainter in his 1988 book *The Collapse of Complex Societies* challenges the idea that environmental degradation causes civilizations to disintegrate. Instead, he points to a scarcity of energy as the common denominator.

Why is there such a dichotomy between two groups who for the most part are arguing for the same thing—the development of alternative energies? We suspect one reason has to do with fringe elements in each group, and especially those who accept the notion of resource depletion. For some in this group, any new energy, even if it's dirty, is a good one. Drilling for oil in national parks or mining the very dirty tar sands of Canada, for instance, is seen as a necessary part of the solution. But environmentalists also are partly to blame.

Most environmentalists accept that we'll need to use fossil fuels in developing renewable energies—it will take fossil fuels, at least initially, to make steel to construct wind turbines, for example. Some, however, see the world purely through a scientific lens that excludes economic variables such as supply and demand and the concept of peak resources. Their climate models suggest that any use of fossil fuels only hastens the day of reckoning. To their way of thinking, the only acceptable energy sources are those that are renewable and/or clean. And they oppose anyone who talks about resource depletion as being either wrong or as making a slippery-slope case that will result in the use of even dirtier sources of energy. They insist that the sole reason to support renewable energies is to clean up the environment.

Policymakers, for the most part, tend to be pragmatic environmentalists. Mainly they ignore the whole topic of resource depletion for fear of alarming the public and instead pay homage to the notion that clean energy is needed to protect our children from the ravages of an unfriendly climate. They focus on how much we need to spend over what period of time.

Perhaps the strongest evidence that this view has prevailed was the awarding of the 2007 Nobel Peace Prize to Al Gore and the Intergovernmental Panel on Climate Change, advocates of dramatic reductions in fossil fuel use and a massive build-out of alternative energies. In effect, the Nobel Committee endorsed the environmental movement, not the peak-resources crowd.

By buying into this movement, the Chinese have positioned themselves to pursue renewable energies in the name of fighting global warming—without ever having to mention resource scarcity. And in fact,

China never mentions peak oil or peak resources in discussing its alternative energy campaign, either in official speeches or in the state-controlled press. Going further, Chinese journalists, speaking anonymously, have told us that there's an unwritten rule that it's off-limits to file stories relating to the country's voracious appetite for natural resources. We think you'd be hard-pressed to even find the phrase "resource scarcity" in any Chinese publication. But it's rare to read a Chinese newspaper without finding a reference to clean energy.

Getting Serious

The Chinese have been backing up their words with strong actions. In the areas of wind, nuclear, solar, and hydropower, the country's growth continues to accelerate. By 2011, or 2012 at the latest, they will hold a leading position in every aspect of renewable energy.

The *Shanghai Daily* has reported that China plans to generate 150 gigawatts from wind energy by 2020, which would be consistent with its 15 percent to 20 percent renewable energy goals. The article went on

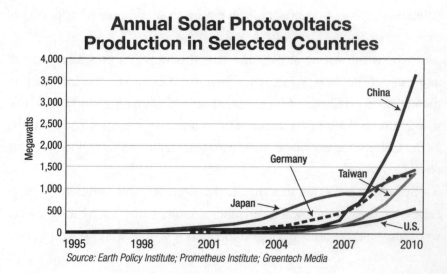

Annual Solar Photovoltaics Production in Selected Countries

Source: Earth Policy Institute; Prometheus Institute; Greentech Media

to add that "the Chinese Renewable Energy Industries Association says it could hit the target far earlier."

The plan would supply the equivalent of more than 800 million tons of coal via renewable sources, according to Liang Zhipeng, head of the New and Renewable Energy division of China's State Energy Bureau. By 2030, renewable energy is expected to account for the equivalent of more than one billion tons of coal, or about 20 percent of China's primary energy consumption. And by 2050, more than one-third of the country's total primary energy consumption—the equivalent of more than two billion tons of coal—is slated to come from renewable energy. Moreover just as the Chinese have made clear that the 15 percent 2020 goal is conservative, so are these goals.

If China achieved its 2020 target, it would mean a 40 to 45 percent reduction in carbon emissions per unit of its GDP from 2005 levels. It's estimated, however, that China's emissions still will nearly double by 2020 if the pace of economic growth matches the past decade's gains. Already the world's biggest carbon polluter, it has no intention of capping its greenhouse gas emissions anytime soon.

Meanwhile, in contrast to China's surging ahead with alternative energies, the United States has barely been inching along. In an article in February 2010, the *Wall Street Journal* documented the frustration being felt by U.S. energy secretary Steven Chu over his inability to spend the $32.7 billion that had been allocated to the development of alternative energy under the stimulus bill. More than a year after the bill's enactment, less than one-tenth of those funds had actually been spent due to a shortage of staff and resources at the Energy Department to evaluate and manage the innovative technologies loan program.

To sum up, we think an ulterior motive is at work in China's seizing the moral high ground on climate change. Their motive has less to do with protecting the environment and more with the desire to acquire increasingly scarce resources. Ignoring this challenge would be a grave mistake for the United States. China's government has been remarkably adept at achieving and even exceeding goals set in past five- and ten-year plans, and there's every reason to believe it will continue to achieve success in the future. Failure on the part of the United States to commit wholeheartedly to a similar crash program before it is too late in this desperately important struggle will irreparably damage our future.

Chapter 3

Peak Oil Has Arrived— and Peak Coal Isn't Far Behind

We argued earlier that there are considerable misunderstandings today as to the underlying drivers of the U.S. economy. The near collapse of the financial sector and the housing crisis, for instance, are seen as the culprits behind the 2008 recession, while high and rising commodity prices are seldom mentioned as anything other than an afterthought. Yet it was the sharp run-up in commodity prices (unrelated to U.S. growth, or speculation) culminating in a spike to nearly $150 a barrel for crude oil that deserves principal recognition—just as sharp increases in energy costs presaged every prior recession since the early 1970s.

As the economy slowed dramatically in late 2008 and early 2009 and unemployment rose to its highest levels in decades, oil prices (along with industrial commodities) came crashing back down—but they didn't stay down for long. This rebound, which was one of the strongest on record and included a doubling in oil prices, was again set in motion by strong demand from emerging economies, namely China. And the impact from soaring commodities on our own economy was very tepid growth, far below what in the past was normal coming out of a recession. Strapped for cash and still reeling from the near double-digit unemployment rate and a dismal housing market, American consumers were also saddled with, among other things, $3 a gallon gasoline, casting a pall over what should have been an optimistic period in the business cycle. But this is the new normal.

Clearly we have no direct control over growth in China and other developing countries. It is also clear that the United States no longer has control over commodity prices. They were the main reason the nation suffered so much in the 2000s. And however horrible the first decade of the twenty-first century was, it's but a prelude of much worse to come.

It follows that a continued rise in commodities—which is certain if we are right on China—will not only lower U.S. economic growth but also hike inflation. That combination is the proverbial rock and a hard place in the extreme. Whatever methods policymakers choose to combat the situation, it won't make any difference as long as China continues to soak up resources—materials that we have long taken for granted. The cycle of ever greater inflation and periodic deflation will repeat and become ever more severe.

Chief among the resources that will make the 2008–09 period look like merely a warm-up is crude oil.

Come Hell or High Water

The *Deepwater Horizon* disaster of the spring of 2010 was a tragic and heartrending ecological catastrophe of epic proportions. Images of oil-soaked pelicans and dead sea turtles, which were already on the endangered species list, washing up on Gulf of Mexico beaches made the blood of even dispassionate viewers boil. And with good reason.

The impact of the worst oil spill in U.S. history will be felt for decades, from both an environmental and an economic standpoint. It's ironic that BP, the company responsible for the spill, has spent hundreds of millions of dollars in recent years to brand itself as "beyond petroleum," for as the tar-stained beaches and vast ocean dead zones in the Gulf attest, its business is anything but green.

More broadly, the spill is evidence of just how desperate our search for oil has become. It is a sign that the world has indeed reached that state of affairs known as "peak oil," which in the past has been disputed, derided, and denied by oil industry executives and politicians in the oil industry's sway.

Peak oil (which we've written about in previous books) in its broadest formulation refers to that point at which demand for oil begins to outstrip the world's ability to supply it. There is lots of oil still left in the ground, including beneath the oceans, and there always will be. But we can no longer pump petroleum fast enough to meet the world's needs. The fact that we've resorted to trying to tap oil that lies miles below the deep ocean's floor, a part of the earth that is as alien and unknown to us as the moon, bespeaks both mind-numbing hubris and true desperation. It tells us we've reached oil's endgame.

When we first began writing about peak oil, it was still a fringe belief. Everyone knew that oil was a finite commodity and that one day it would cease being available in the amounts required. But the consensus was that such a day of reckoning was many decades, even as much as a century, away. Such assurances were useful to oil company executives who had no interest in the world moving away from its dependence on oil.

Back then, pretty much the only people talking about peak oil were academics, who drew on the work of a few far-thinking geologists. There was a lot of statistical analysis showing how quickly oilfields become depleted and estimating how much oil existed beneath the earth's surface. But these discussions had a theoretical cast and lacked urgency.

Today, though, peak oil is no longer a fringe belief, and it's no longer a mere academic matter. It has moved into mainstream thought, widely accepted by scientists and publicly acknowledged by an expanding roster of top oil industry executives, and it's immensely relevant to all our lives because our economy, indeed our entire way of life, is predicated on cheap energy. And there is no viable, portable substitute that comes anywhere close to packing the tremendous energy density of oil.

A one-word reason accounts for the change: China.

China's need for oil has vastly accelerated the peak oil day of reckoning. China is the world's second-largest consumer of oil behind the United States, even with its per capita consumption far less than our own. And there's no end in sight to that country's growing demand. If it weren't for China, peak oil might still be viewed as an academic sideshow. But now the reality of peak oil has become widely accepted and exists in the here and now. It has moved beyond theoretical discussions in a few ivory tower halls of academia to the mainstream of scientific and industrial thought.

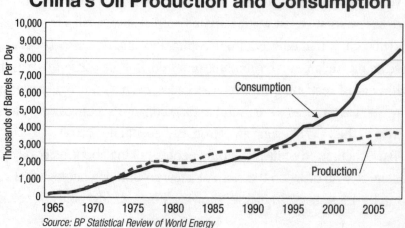

China's Oil Production and Consumption

Source: BP Statistical Review of World Energy

And though it's still not front-page news yet, the subject is cropping up in media reports with increasing frequency.

Nevertheless, peak oil has yet to permeate the consciousness of the American population at large. There are still many who believe we can drill our way into ensuring we have enough oil for generations to come, and put off the need for a large-scale shift to energy alternatives to the future. Consequently, the United States is still failing to treat the development of alternatives as the vital imperative that it is. And we're therefore still not focusing on what resources we will need and on how we can ensure that we will have enough of them.

And here's the troubling part: We're not—but China is.

Forty-Year Warning

For its energy needs, the United States, like Blanche DuBois in *A Streetcar Named Desire*, has long relied on the kindness of strangers (many of whom harbor ill will toward us and our way of life). Our country now relies on imports to supply two-thirds of its oil needs, up from about one-third in the mid-1980s. Contrary to the stated beliefs of a few politicians and some conservative talk show hosts, captured in clever sound bites for mass consumption, the United States can never drill its way to energy independence. Period. And anyone who thinks otherwise is as delusional as Blanche in Tennessee Williams' play.

While China is pressing forward with utmost speed to build an alternative energy economy, the United States muddles along, merely paying lip service to the idea. Instead, our national policy is echoed in the misguided chant, "Drill, baby, drill." Yet we've used up most of the easy-to-acquire oil, forcing us to go to extreme lengths in search of new deposits.

U.S. crude oil production peaked in 1970, according to Department of Energy data. Although we enjoyed a brief upturn in production with the development of Alaska's North Slope in the late 1970s, the slide resumed a few years later. The oil industry's move into Gulf of Mexico production did slow the descent in output, but the trend has still been relentlessly downward. Nor will drilling on the outer continental shelf, which President Obama was willing to allow for the first time just days before the BP catastrophe, stop this production contraction.

Of the oil we do still produce, a growing share comes from deepwater drilling. Yet there's good reason to believe we're sowing the seeds of our own economic ruin through this dependence on offshore oil. Just a decade ago, deepwater drilling accounted for around 15 percent of our production; today it comprises more than 30 percent.

Worldwide, the story is much the same. Like Texas and Alaska, one oil-producing region after another has eventually gone into terminal decline: Indonesia, the North Sea, Mexico, Russia...the list goes on. And while these areas will continue to produce oil for many years to come, the dramatic rates of decline in production once past peak have been alarming, forcing companies to look for oil in ever more challenging areas.

It's no understatement to say these searches for new oil are acts of desperation. We're exploring in places that only a few years ago were considered technically unreachable and financially too risky. Adjusted for inflation, the average cost of drilling a new oil well (both on land and off-shore) has risen more than fivefold in the past decade. And as we painfully learned with the BP spill, the risks of drilling in these new frontiers still aren't fully recognized.

The deepwater ocean floor is an area so remote that mankind has very little understanding of it. In other words, there is no way to properly assess the probability of an accident or calculate the damage that would be caused if there is an accident. It is almost like searching for oil on the moon—except on the moon we might have a better chance of quantifying damages.

BP's Macondo blowout was an unfortunate example of what can happen when you drill many thousands of feet into the ocean floor. What's more, it is a mistake to treat such an accident as a one-off event. There is a massive difference between a low-probability event and a complete fluke. For example, even if the chance of such an accident is only 1 in 100, if you repeat that process 1,000 times then the chance of such an accident becomes nearly certain—99.996 percent assured. Moreover, the ability to model what the cost of such an accident will be is essentially zero. Yet for all the danger such drilling entails, hunting for new oil reserves far below the ocean is the only way the world can temporarily maintain even close to adequate oil supplies. Even for us to stay at a steady level of supply requires new drilling to make up for the roughly four million barrels a year lost due to depletion among existing oilfields. So it's a marathon in which we have to run faster and farther each year just to stay in place. But we're now at or at best very near the limits of our endurance.

Consider another BP oil platform in the Gulf of Mexico, *Thunder Horse*. The $1 billion platform was part of one of the most expensive drilling projects in the world, designed to process 250,000 barrels of oil a day. But it has been plagued from the start. After numerous engineering problems and severe damage as a result of Hurricane Katrina, *Thunder Horse* finally came online in 2008. The oilfield, however, reached its maximum output of just 172,000 barrels per day the following year, after which production started to decline. The rig's production has since collapsed, and as of this writing, output is down to around 50,000 barrels a day, in part due to "maintenance issues," though BP has been tight-lipped as to what those are. It now appears that *Thunder Horse* will never come close to producing the billion barrels it promised at the outset.

Keep in mind that an offshore oil platform is expensive to maintain. Investors demand a high initial return on their investment, since the wells don't have a "long tail" production life like the stripper wells that dot the West Texas landscape, which can pump out as little as a few barrels a day for decades. So in addition to more disasters like *Deepwater Horizon*, we're likely to encounter more expensive disappointments along the lines of *Thunder Horse* as we seek out oil deep below the ocean floor. What's more, we're likely to find that the actual reserves from these wells can be far less than anticipated, thus raising the per-barrel cost even higher.

When, Not If

The notion that we need to develop alternative energies, that fossil fuels—oil, coal, and natural gas—are not long-term solutions to powering the world's economies, is something almost everyone accepts, though a few diehards still believe the world contains a virtually inexhaustible amount of oil. But it's clear that emerging economies of more than five billion people can't keep developing at a burgeoning rate unless they develop alternative energies. If anything, the recent recession proved how close we are to peak energy, in that during the worst economic crisis since World War II, we experienced only a modest drop in global demand and a quick rebound in energy prices.

At this juncture, the only debate is whether the peak has already occurred or will occur within the next few years. We have detailed much data for the growing scarcity of oil in previous books and won't go into great detail here, as this information hasn't changed. Indeed, it continues to pile up in favor of the growing scarcity of fossil fuels.

Peak oil doesn't mean we're about to run out of petroleum, but it does mean the flow rates of oil production will inexorably decline. We are at the end of cheap oil. Many in the United States, however, see this as a distant concern that really doesn't need to be addressed until some point in the future. But China recognizes the threat for what it is and is acting accordingly.

China is actively, if quietly, preparing for this imminent crisis today. It is gearing up for a fight for survival, not just by securing future oil and natural gas flows from far-flung nations—including some run by the world's most despicable despots—but also by spending a considerable portion of the nation's GDP erecting wind and solar power generating capacity. And it is scrambling to ensure supplies of key metals and minerals essential for future alternative energy construction while those resources are still relatively abundant and inexpensive. So the battle lines are being drawn, yet to its great peril America remains essentially unmindful of the looming threat, fixated instead on the here and now.

Following the peak in crude oil, the world will be using ever greater quantities of energy to extract the remaining oil reserves. And since we live in an interrelated world, as oil prices rise we will pay more for extracting iron ore, copper, nickel, and all the rest, which in turn will drive up the cost of oil production. Rinse and repeat. At a certain point, the cost of lifting a barrel of oil out of the ground will exceed the marginal utility of that oil.

Sure, producers keep finding more oil, and we've become quite skillful in extracting oil left behind in fields once thought to be played out. But the added reserves and flow rates from these sources aren't coming close to replacing the oil the world is consuming.

Data from the International Energy Agency (IEA) shows that while July 2008—at the onset of the financial crisis—was the peak month in oil production, 2005 was the peak *year* of conventional oil production. This despite rising oil prices that traditional economic models would have us believe should lead to new discoveries to offset the decline. The IEA has historically been overly optimistic with its forecasts, but now admits we're headed for trouble. In its *World Energy Outlook 2010* the organization forecast that "crude oil output reaches an undulating plateau of around 68–69 million barrels a day by 2020, but never regains its all time peak of 70 million barrels a day reached in 2006." The IEA then went on to pin its hopes on oil yet to be found to make up for the expected 80 percent decline in conventional oil out to 2035. It also looks for production of natural gas liquids and unconventional oil to grow strongly to meet rising demand, which likewise seems overly hopeful.

Globally, we have seen an increase in oil production in recent years only by stretching the definition of oil to include such sources as the

Alberta tar sands, natural gas liquids, and biofuels such as ethanol. Each of these, however, has limitations, and none are a long-term panacea for declining production of conventional oil.

Producing one barrel of synthetic crude oil from the Fort McMurray tar sands, for instance, requires mining two tons of sand that must be processed using 250 gallons of water and 1,400 cubic feet of natural gas, in the course of which is emitted 240 pounds of carbon dioxide (three times more than conventional oil production). So extracting oil from tar sands is likely to contribute only moderately to the world's future energy needs. The water required alone has already become an issue and simply isn't available in sufficient quantity for a sizable scaling up in production. It also makes no sense to use clean-burning natural gas to make synthetic crude oil.

The adoption of ethanol does have a straightforward appeal with American consumers, but it simply doesn't scale either. If our entire national corn crop were used to make ethanol, it would replace only a small fraction of our oil consumption. Indeed, using all of the green plants in the United States—crops, grasslands, and forests—wouldn't come close to doing the job.

In recent years the major oil companies, eager to make up for dwindling reserves, have turned to unconventional sources of hydrocarbons. Today the rush is into unconventional natural gas locked up in shale deposits. On the surface it's easy to see the attractiveness of pursuing shale gas. Oil finds are becoming increasingly scarce, and in size they have mostly been confined to hard-to-get areas such as the deep waters of the Gulf of Mexico and off the coast of Brazil. In contrast, natural gas is readily being found right in the United States, thanks to horizontal drilling and chemical and hydraulic fracturing, or "fracking," that give drillers maximized access to the gas contained in tight rock formations. The use of these techniques has led to a sharp increase in estimates of U.S. gas reserves.

In addition to being seemingly abundant in the United States, natural gas is alluring because it's much cleaner-burning than coal and releases far less CO_2 into the atmosphere when it's consumed. Coal usage isn't going away, but with global warming on everyone's mind, natural gas is likely to be in high demand. Unfortunately, shale gas fields tend to play out quickly (production drops off by as much as 65 percent in the first year). Plus, over the long haul, the likely cost of extracting the gas, in terms of energy required, for water injected, and for other resources such as transporting the gas, is likely to be high.

In a Far Country

Depletion and increased energy consumption are worries not just of the developed world On April 27, 2010, Khalid al-Falih, chief executive of Saudi Aramco, the state-run oil company, made an alarming statement that went largely unnoticed. He pointed out that the kingdom's domestic energy *demand* was expected to rise from the equivalent of about 3.4 million barrels of crude per day (bpd) to about 8.3 million bpd by 2028.

Surging energy demand from emerging economies is nothing new; it's a pattern the world has witnessed time and again during the past fifty years. In Asia, for instance, Japan, South Korea, Taiwan, and now China,

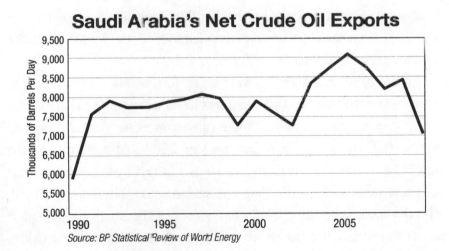

Saudi Arabia's Net Crude Oil Exports

Source: BP Statistical Review of World Energy

all experienced it as their economies matured and income levels rose. In the past this wasn't a problem as the world's producers were able to add to capacity. The quandary is that this time around the world is bumping up against the limits of its oil production capabilities.

But if Saudi Arabia—the world's best hope for rising oil production—is at or near the peak in its production, as there's every reason to believe, its impact on the world will be massive. And the problem will be compounded by the Saudis' growing domestic consumption of oil, which means there will be even less available for export.

If you haven't followed the pronouncements from the Saudi kingdom, suffice to say they never understate how much oil they have in reserve. We should be scared to death, but instead their pronouncements do not even make the nightly news in America. Not many years ago the kingdom was promising that pumping 20 million barrels a day was a conservative projection. Now it looks like we'll be lucky to get 12 million a day. And even that level is suspect.

In April 2008, the official Saudi Press Agency reported that King Abdullah had given orders that some new oil discoveries should be left untapped to preserve the nation's oil wealth. "I keep no secret from you that when there were some new finds, I told them, 'No, leave it in the ground, with grace from God, our children need it.'" Coupled with earlier statements designed to lower expectations, this hardly sounds like a nation blessed with 260 billion barrels of reserves, enough to meet the world's needs for decades to come, as it had once claimed.

In July 2010, King Abdullah went a step further. Speaking to a group of university students, he ordered a halt to oil exploration to save oil for future generations. "I was heading a cabinet meeting and told them to pray to God the Almighty to give it a long life. I told them that I have ordered a halt to all oil explorations so part of this wealth is left for our sons and successors, God willing," he said. A senior oil ministry official, who declined to be named, later indicated that the king's proclamation wasn't an outright ban but rather meant that future exploration activities should be carried out wisely. The king's remarks came just a month after Aramco's annual review proudly proclaimed, "We operate an extensive and aggressive exploration program to ensure we will have the petroleum resources to meet domestic and world demand for many years to come."

One glaring sign that Saudi Aramco is scrambling just to maintain its production, never mind increase it, is its exploration efforts in the Red Sea, far from known oil and gas deposits in the eastern region of the country and the shallow Persian Gulf. The Red Sea can reach depths in excess of a mile and is geologically challenging in that beneath the sea floor is a salt layer 7,000 feet thick. It's extremely difficult both to get good seismic data below the salt layer and to punch a drill bit through. The state-run company also has no deepwater drilling experience. Ali Al Hauwaj, the Saudi Aramco manager responsible for this exploration effort, has admitted that "exploring the Red Sea is just like going to another country." So why, if we are to believe the Saudis' oft-repeated claims that they can raise production dramatically from existing oilfields, are they hunting for reserves in "another country"?

So the next time someone tells you that oil production is not a concern thanks to all the oil deep off the coasts of the United States, Brazil, West Africa, and elsewhere, remind them that finding that oil may be akin to jumping out of an airplane without a parachute to avoid being caught by someone chasing you. Also tell him that if he survives the jump, it won't make much difference because even if these deep wells are successful they are only stopgaps. All too soon, even the oil from deep beneath the ocean won't be enough. America and the rest of the world's economies have got to start employing—on a massive scale—alternative energies or else face the continued dramatic loss in our quality of life.

Trying to Avoid an Unhappy Ending

Interestingly, while the spill in the Gulf of Mexico was unfolding in early spring 2010, another crisis also in the news was having a greater effect on financial markets. That was the crisis with the euro. Greek profligacy had been a catalyst for a dramatic sell-off not only in Greek bonds but also in the bonds of other countries in Europe with large deficits such as Portugal and Spain. The euro was falling fast and furiously, and markets across the globe, fearing an implosion in the large European economy, were dropping like stones.

The Europeans (hardly known for their abiding friendships) did manage to get together and craft a massive bailout approaching a trillion dollars. The bailout was able to overwhelm the markets—or, more precisely, keep speculators from destroying the bond markets of those weak European countries.

The reason we bring this up is that it clearly illustrates a distinction we have always made—between a problem that can be solved by money and one that cannot. The European crisis, at least over the short term, fell into the former, while the energy problem—even a microcosm of it, the spill in the Gulf of Mexico—did not. Notice we say short term, because in the longer term no amount of money can create a Europe that can remain united around a single currency. Among other things, that would require that the French and Germans bury several centuries of antipathy, and that Greeks work as hard as Germans.

In the Gulf, even a trillion dollars could not have guaranteed success any more than trillions of dollars could guarantee a successful journey to Mars. Not even trillions of dollars is necessarily enough to solve the nearly intractable.

Here is a simple analogy. If you are of able body and spirit and need a change of scenery and have the money, you can just hop on an airplane and take a trip to the Caribbean. If you are lying in bed with a broken back and want a change, all you can do is pray that you will heal. Right now America is praying, or should be praying, that it wakes up before spiraling commodity prices—and in particular energy prices—make travel and many other things we associate with our way of life impossible. And the problems America faces today are ones that cannot be solved by money. As we will show in later chapters, all the money in the world (and we don't mean just currency but gold too) will not be able to solve the overwhelming problem facing America. This predicament is a fundamental scarcity of commodities without which we can no longer live as we have.

Indeed, we seem blind to how difficult high commodity prices have already made things for Americans. The first decade of this century was by some measures the worst ever for many financial assets, including stocks. Economic growth during the decade was the lowest since the 1930s, and returns on stocks were negative. Even during the 1930s and 1970s stocks eked out positive returns. Median salaries in the country dropped by the most since at least the 1930s. What did rise in the 2000s were resources. Despite the massive dip in most resource prices during the economic debacle, on balance resource prices had one of their best decades ever. Oil prices, for example, climbed about fourfold.

Flying commodities served as a fierce headwind for the economy, and were also a catalyst for the worst economic crisis since the Great Depression. One thing to realize about rising oil is that it is an unqualified negative for the economy, and the same is true for any other resource that we import for a great deal of our needs. Rising oil is a tax on our economy. Remember $1.50 gasoline? Gone forever. Also gone forever is the difference between what you are paying now and the $1.50 per gallon you used to pay. In other words, rising resource prices act as a tax on all of us. But this is not your old-fashioned friendly tax, the one the government imposes to raise money to pay for military expenditures, education, or just to pay down the deficit. Those kinds of taxes are as likely to aid the economy as to slow things down. Defense spending, for example, can increase high-paying jobs. Those kinds of taxes also tend to reduce inflation. But that's hardly true with rising resource prices, which push up inflation. It makes all the difference in the world if rising gasoline prices go into government coffers or a bunch of sheiks' pockets. And that brings us to the summer of 2008.

Both America and Europe were in a recession, but at the same time inflation in both economies was on the rise. This unhappy state of affairs came about courtesy of oil prices close to $150 a barrel. At that time—which now seems a lifetime ago—central bankers viewed their primary job as to be inflation fighters. In August 2008, about a month before Lehman Brothers was to become the first domino in a chain reaction that nearly destroyed capitalism in a deflationary conflagration, our Federal Reserve was debating whether or not to *raise* interest rates in an attempt to curb inflation. This is not too different from considering whether you should douse a fire with gasoline. And while our Fed demurred, the European Central Bank, at the urging of Germany, actually increased rates.

The rest is history—but unfortunately a history that is likely to repeat itself... again and again. Not only is 2008 unlikely to be a one-off event, but its next rendition is likely to be more severe. And while we await the next full-scale calamity, it seems certain that the American way of life will continue to deteriorate.

Consider if you could travel in a time machine back to 2000 and were to ask fifty leading economists to predict the price of oil a decade hence, assuming the United States did not increase its consumption of oil and if the unemployment rate were to approximate 10 percent. Obviously we can't do that experiment in real life, but we doubt that any honest person would argue with an answer of oil below $20 a barrel. And no one would have believed that gasoline prices would be much above $1.25 a gallon. Instead, many would maintain that gas would cost less than a dollar under such conditions.

Today's prices are clearly out of whack and without a doubt a consequence of growing scarcity of oil and other resources. Clearly the market is sending up a warning signal that few are yet heeding. With these scarcities likely to grow and even accelerate in the years ahead, our way of life and the returns on our financial investments are likely to continue their decline. Worse still, that decline is more likely to accelerate than level off.

As we saw in 2008 when oil prices were approaching $150 a barrel, even a modest gap between supply and demand for a commodity can send prices soaring. As we move beyond peak oil, that gap will widen substantially, causing energy prices to soar far above what most people can imagine. And it won't stop with just oil.

Next Up ... Peak Coal

In many circles, the debate on "peak oil" remains unsettled, despite mounting evidence that it's here and now. At the same time, conventional wisdom holds that there are ample coal supplies to meet the world's needs for decades, if not centuries, to come. This supposition, however, is usually taken on blind faith. Upon close examination, the world may be close to "peak coal" as well. That is not to say we're running out of coal, but that we may be very near its peak in terms of its energy content, measured in British thermal units (BTUs).

Coal currently supplies about 30 percent of the world's primary energy needs, behind oil (at around 35 percent) and ahead of natural gas (at 24 percent). The combined energy generated from wind and solar, incidentally, amounts to less than 0.005 percent of the world's total energy

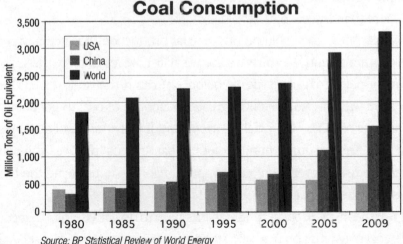

Coal Consumption

Source: BP Statistical Review of World Energy

consumption. Meanwhile, the U.S. Energy Information Agency, which historically has generated overly optimistic production forecasts, expects that annual coal production will climb 15 percent by 2035. That's a tall order.

Coal production is in decline for most countries around the world. Nations such as Germany, the United Kingdom, Ukraine, and Poland, all once important coal miners, must now supplement their own production with imports.

Today, coal mining is dominated by just five countries: the United States, Russia, China, Australia, and India, which together possess nearly 80 percent of the world's known reserves. Of these, only Australia, Russia, and the United States make a significant portion of their output available for export. They're joined by a handful of others, including Indonesia, Colombia, Kazakhstan, and South Africa, as top actors on the export stage, though at its current pace Indonesia will essentially exhaust its reserves sometime in the next decade.

The United States is believed to contain nearly 29 percent of the world's remaining reserves, or some 245 years' worth at current production rates. So it would seem we're immune from any dislocation that might occur in the coal market. This reserve estimate, however, is grossly misleading in that the BTU content of the coal we mine has been in decline for more than a decade.

Though the total volume of U.S. coal production may actually climb for another twenty to thirty years, we will have essentially passed the point of peak coal domestically before we reach that milestone. Thereafter, we will have to burn ever greater quantities of coal to generate the same level of BTUs, which will shorten considerably the life of our unused reserves. And of course, mining these remaining coal reserves will necessitate the use of ever more energy, presumably coal, reducing the life of those reserves further.

But the most disconcerting statistics have to do with China. That country's coal consumption rose by a staggering 134 percent in the first decade of this century. In 1999 China consumed only about 20 percent more coal than the United States; a decade later its usage was three times that of the United States. Despite being home to the world's third largest coal reserves, China has also recently been forced to become a net importer of coal in order to satisfy its voracious appetite.

China's need is largely the reason U.S. coking coal prices rose from around $40 a ton in 2000 to $180 a ton in 2008—a four-and-a-half-fold rise—before the financial crisis prompted a retreat to around $120 a ton. And it's why coal prices are destined to soar far higher in the years to come.

China is currently burning nearly half of the world's annual coal production. At its current rate of growth, the country's demand will soon soak up every available ton on the export market. Put another way, between the end of 2009 and 2015, China will likely need additional coal supplies equivalent to between three to four Australias—not just the equivalent of what Australia exports, but its entire coal output.

Even if China is successful in producing 15 to 20 percent of its primary power from renewable sources in 2020, the country's consumption of coal will continue to grow at an alarming rate, as the Chinese economy is likely to continue to expand at an impressive tempo, as it has for the past sixty-plus years.

Despite its having the world's third largest reserves, though, China's coal deposits are expected to last only for another thirty-eight years based on 2009 production figures. Yet as with the remaining life of U.S. coal reserves, this is an overly simplistic way of viewing those reserves, which understates the dire nature of what is already a critical state of affairs.

Reinforcing this view are several independent studies of the world's troubled coal situation. For instance, a 2007 study by the Energy Watch Group, a Germany-based organization of independent scientists and parliamentarians, saw coal peaking by 2020. It pointed out that reserve data worldwide is of poor quality—in some cases it has not been revised in decades. In the case of China, the country's reserve estimates have not changed since 1992. As a result, many estimates greatly overstate the amount of coal yet to be mined. Based on a country-by-country analysis, the group concluded that global production would still increase by around 30 percent over the following ten to fifteen years. However, the production profile of the world's largest producer, China, would determine the peak of global coal production. And after 2020 the Energy Watch Group study estimated that global coal production would decline sharply.

Two years later, in 2009, researchers at the China Center for Energy Economics Research published an article in the journal *Energy Policy* that came to a similar conclusion, that peak coal production in China would occur around 2030. This is not some fringe group reaching this conclusion but scientists from Xiamen University in Fujian, one of China's top institutions.

The researchers saw that the gap between China's internal supply and demand would continue to grow and the gap would have to be made up with increased imports. They estimated, "By 2015, the volume of net coal imports to China would account for 11–34 percent of the world coal trade and by 2030 that would be 41–54 percent, as predicted. That means that about 50 percent of the total world coal would be traded with China. If this is the case, a slight change in China's coal market would have a great impact on international coal markets, especially on international coal prices."

It would appear by the country's actions since this study was published that its conclusions did not escape the attention of the Chinese government. Given that coal accounts for 70 percent of Chinese energy use, it follows that the country would be somewhat frantic to develop alternative sources of energy. Concerned that it is drawing down its remaining coal reserves at an alarming rate, the government is now considering capping domestic coal production, according to reports from China's state-run media.

In the meantime, the impact on the world market of China importing increasing quantities of coal is already being felt, although we've experienced just a taste of what's in store. In essence, this rise in coal prices is taking money out of the pockets of Americans and, indeed, consumers the world over, leaving us less to spend on other things.

As we'll show in the following chapters, there are a wide range of commodities that are destined to skyrocket in the near future along with oil and coal with their supply unable to keep up with demand.

What can we do? Clearly the first thing to ponder is what the Chinese have not only been thinking about for years but are now employing in overdrive. We mean the development of renewable energies, or any energy source that can substitute for oil and, increasingly, coal.

Chapter 4

Blind to Copper Realities

We Americans just don't get it. Nothing better illustrates our ignorance of—or complacency about—the threats to our civilization than the wars we have been fighting in Iraq and Afghanistan. Some observers, such as Nobel Prize–winning economist Joseph Stiglitz, estimate that these wars have cost the American economy more than $3 trillion. These efforts have also cost us in terms of lost service personnel, as well as untold resources and opportunities to develop critical resources. Indeed, a sizable chunk of the $3 trillion estimate comes from the oil used to fight the war and the concomitant rise in oil prices. Three trillion dollars spent on developing renewable energies might obviate the need for writing this book.

But the war costs—even larger ones—would not be so critical were it not for the fact that they have given China carte blanche to develop those same critical resources that the entire world will need but that there are not nearly enough of to go around. We will focus primarily on copper in this chapter, as it is the scarcest of the major metals. But we will also make clear that what goes for copper is also true for most metals. And what goes is that China is rapidly accumulating a lion's share of these metals, which will deprive us of a chance to develop renewable energies.

Perhaps Afghanistan is the best illustration of the critical differences between China and America and why even if America wins the proverbial battle in Afghanistan it will lose the war in spades. However noble our aspirations in Afghanistan, they are meaningless if they lead us down a road where we simply don't have the energy to run our economy, and for that matter to fight further wars. If we emerge even wholly victorious in Afghanistan, the war will most likely be the ultimate Pyrrhic victory.

While we have been spending many billions of dollars fighting in Afghanistan, risking the lives of our service personnel and supporting a corrupt regime in a land that the Russians failed to conquer in the twentieth century and the British were chased out of in the nineteenth century, the Chinese are quietly invading Afghanistan as well. But whereas we've sent combat troops and have little to show for it, since 2007 China has openly marched into the country with an army of geologists, mining experts, and engineers and is walking away with immense wealth in what is arguably the most critical of all major metals, copper.

China Metallurgical Group Corporation, a state-owned conglomerate, paid $3.4 billion for the rights to a deposit located in a former al-Qaeda stronghold south of Kabul that is believed to contain 13 million (and perhaps as much as 20 million) tons of copper. Most striking about the transaction, the price tag was a staggering $1 billion above bids from U.S., Canadian, Russian, and Kazakh companies. And the deal, according to a November 19, 2009, *Washington Post* article, was sealed with a $30 million bribe paid to the Afghan mining minister, something the Chinese see as just a part of the cost of doing business, but which is illegal for Western companies.

The Aynak copper field, as it is known, contains the equivalent of more than a third of China's known copper reserves. When full-scale operations commence in 2014, it will be one of the biggest foreign investment projects in the history of Afghanistan. A poor country to begin with, after more than thirty years of war Afghanistan has virtually no infrastructure in place to speak of. For the Chinese, this means starting entirely from scratch.

In addition to the mine itself, the company is constructing a smelter to refine the copper ore and a 400-megawatt power plant to run both the mine and smelter. It's also establishing a coal mine to supply fuel for the power station generator, and it is building rail lines to bring the coal to the power plant and to ship the refined copper back to China. The entire operation will ultimately employ around ten thousand people, but for now the work is mostly being carried out by Chinese nationals behind barbed-wire fences and fortified positions, with a private Chinese security force watching over them—not to mention the security provided by the armed forces of the United States and its allies.

The People's Republic is willing to take on the security risk of operating in Afghanistan. Why? Because it is going to need every last pound of copper from the Aynak mine and much more in the next few years if the country is to succeed in its efforts for the wide-scale development of alternative energy.

Copper at this writing is trading at about $4.50 a pound, which is very expensive by historical norms but still relatively cheap as a contributor to the cost of most items for which it is used. The metal is clearly not on our government's list of critical metals that should be stockpiled. But copper's growing scarcity virtually guarantees that its price will vault into the stratosphere—crimping our ability to build homes, windmills, high-voltage cables, and hybrid cars. In other words, without relatively cheap copper our entire economy will be turned upside down. The Chinese—by their actions in Afghanistan, by their hoarding of every scrap of copper—clearly grasp not only the metal's importance but unlike America are keenly aware of its growing scarcity.

Copper's prospective scarcity should not have been a secret to Americans. In January 2006 Yale professors Gordon, Bertram, and Graedel penned "Metal Stocks and Sustainability" for the prestigious *Proceedings of the National Academy of Science*. Part of their conclusions reads as follows:

Concern about the extent of mineral resources arises when the stock of metal needed to provide the services enjoyed by the highly developed nations is compared with that needed to provide comparable services with existing technology to a large part of the world's population. Our stock data demonstrate that current technologies would require the entire copper and zinc ore resource in the lithosphere and perhaps that of platinum as well.

Back in 2006 these may have sounded like theoretical musings from a trio of academics. The only thing that was theoretical is that the time scale is much shorter than anyone had ever imagined and the list of major metals (we will discuss the minor metals in the next chapter) that are becoming scarce has grown at an almost exponential rate. It is not just copper, zinc, and platinum, but also silver and, remarkably—despite its seeming abundance—even iron ore. Keep in mind that no material can be extracted without energy and that energy cannot be extracted without using metals. These interrelationships, which were discussed at length in a previous book, *Game Over* (2009), are a major reason that energy-intensive iron ore has to be regarded as scarce. Yet the scarcity of major everyday metals is far removed from almost all Americans' perspective.

The largest mining company in the world is Australia-based BHP Billiton. They have leading positions in everything from copper to coal to zinc to iron ore. In a recent presentation of their yearly results, they included a chart of various metals and commodities, which they measured in terms of prospective scarcity. Specifically they asked, at current demand levels and estimates of the world's current reserves, how much remains of a particular metal or commodity? For oil, the answer was forty-one years, the same as nickel. For copper, the answer was thirty years.

Copper, therefore, is much scarcer than oil. And oil, as we pointed out earlier, is close to reaching a peak—the point at which potential increases in production are no longer going to be sufficient to supply potential increases in demand. Though much less work has been done on copper, it should surprise no one if copper was also at a peak—or even past its peak.

One critical question is when will America join the Chinese and notice that copper has become so scarce. The best answer we have comes from a comment a friend made regarding oil. He noted that a bullish outlook on copper was just a trade recommendation, whereas a bullish outlook on oil was a macro statement. Consider that over $2.5 trillion of oil is traded every year, which is several percent of total world economic product. This numbers dwarfs the $100 billion that is traded in copper. Copper is barely a rounding error in the world's economic output. And this means that this rare metal, though vital, is not a big enough part of the cost in even critical products to get much attention.

For the sake of example, let's say copper represents 5 percent of the cost of a house and the metal then doubles in price. That is not really a big deal, as copper will still represent less than 10 percent of the total cost. But what happens if copper rises tenfold? Then all of a sudden it becomes more than 30 percent of the cost of the house—assuming, of course, that other costs hold constant. Our example is what is likely to happen on a worldwide scale. Scarcity plus irreplaceable critical uses virtually assures that prices will rise to the point where copper will become a "macro" metal.

Just as oil has become so expensive that in America we have stopped increasing our use of it, the same thing will happen to copper. But in the case of copper (and, of course, oil) the day of reckoning comes when we realize we desperately need these materials to build out an alternative energy infrastructure. Then prices rise to the point where copper prices take an ever-growing bite out of our incomes and our economy is jolted again and again by the rising cost of the red metal.

Sound unreal? Well, then go back to America in the 1950s, when oil was trading for a few bucks a barrel. Who would have believed that this fuel, which was then so abundant in America, would one day become the focus of the world's attention? Back then there was even a television commercial that encouraged the use of electricity, with the slogan, "Electricity costs less today than it did twenty-five years ago." It was a mistake to take fossil fuels for granted back then, and today it is a mistake to take virtually any material for granted.

Noteworthy is that even a presumed abundant supply of a metal does not assure that it will be available for an indefinite time. One reason is that in estimates such as BHP's, even those metals or commodities with estimated long lives are not necessarily guaranteed to be available in sufficient quantity for even a relatively short period of time. Coal, for example, which we discussed in a previous chapter, has an estimated life expectancy of 147 years in the BHP table. But as the Chinese and others have pointed out, the day of peak coal is less than a generation away. (The two largest developing countries, China and India, are already net importers of coal.) One reason for the discrepancy is that demand will not remain constant—which is the assumption underlying the number of years left in BHP's calculation—but will likely grow very rapidly. The other is the theoretical nature of the projections. In all cases, the mining of reserves becomes much more intensive after you have already mined a large portion of the original endowment.

Known Recoverable World Resource Reserves at Current Demand Levels

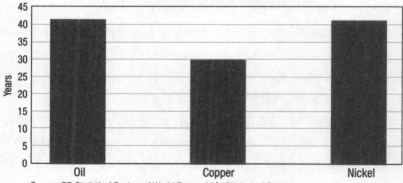

Source: BP Statistical Review of World Energy, U.S. Geological Survey

Indeed, the basic relation that holds true with oil also applies to many other metals. Once you have mined about half of what was originally there, increasing the amount mined becomes ever more difficult. Even BHP's estimate of platinum reserves lasting three hundred years is not meaningful, primarily because enough platinum has already been mined to assure that future mining will become ever more expensive and difficult. Indeed, the Yale professors we referred to above who wrote about the potential scarcity of metals had platinum on their short list. As more of a mineral is mined, the grade (the amount you find in a ton of dirt) starts to diminish rapidly. In the case of coal, instead of decreasing in terms of grade, it decreases in terms of energy content (BTUs). Though America, for example, has not mined half its endowment of coal, likely it has already mined more than half the BTUs of the original endowment. This is one reason that the Chinese are so desperate to develop alternative energies, in spite of the long-lived estimates for coal. The coal that currently remains in the lithosphere is of lesser quality than that already mined and the quality (energy content) continues to decline.

Obstacles in the Path to a Sustainable Future

The reason the day of reckoning for scarce metals is drawing closer much faster than anyone imagined as recently as five or six years ago is, of course, the need for renewable fuels. Without copper, without zinc, without silver, without iron ore, without many other metals, the building of an economy reliant on renewable energies is simply impossible.

Mark Jacobson, a professor at Stanford University, deserves credit for being ahead of the curve on renewable energies. In the early 2000s he wrote a seminal article in *Science* magazine arguing that electricity generated from wind was cheaper than all other forms of electricity. Events have clearly proved him correct, or at least partially so, as wind has become the renewable energy of choice. Since that article Jacobson has gone on to argue that the world could rely almost entirely on wind for its energy needs—not just electricity but all energy. In a subsequent article in *Science* he argued that wind electrolysis was a cheaper way of producing a transportation energy carrier (hydrogen) than is refining gasoline from oil. These studies on wind were all peer-reviewed and discussed in online forums. In our opinion, Jacobson's points held up very well.

Jacobson, however, is much more an environmentalist than someone concerned with resource scarcity. We think that is one reason why a number of his arguments, though they have received a lot of press, have still not gotten their full due. He talks in terms of twenty- or thirty-year intervals rather than stressing the urgency of the present. It is tragic that these two worlds can't meet. One of his latest contributions shows why.

Jacobson along with a colleague wrote a cover story in the November 2009 issue of *Scientific American* that provided a presumed road map for a world that was fossil fuel–free by the year 2030. The three sources of renewable energies that Jacobson picked were—in order of importance— wind, solar, and hydroelectric. While he did not dismiss other energies, he argued that these three were the cleanest and the most abundant and easily applied.

Ironically, upon analysis this article, rather than being a road map to a renewable future, provides compelling reasons why a world of renewable energies is no longer possible. Jacobson estimates that the cost of the renewable energy platform will be $100 trillion (not including transmission costs, which we assume would be at least another $20 trillion).

Let's just stop for a moment at these estimates—approximately $120 trillion (which we will argue below is conservative). Consider this number in relation to how much copper is available for mining. According to the U.S. Geological Survey, there are 630 million tons of copper reserves—copper that is considered to be minable under current economic conditions. At current prices the value of all that copper if it were suddenly made available would be about $5.7 trillion, which is less than 5 percent of the projected cost to segue from nonrenewable energies to renewable energies.

Some may argue that we should use resources—the estimated total amount of copper available in the lithosphere—as our measure of potential copper supply. This number has been estimated to be about three billion tons, a much bigger number, but still one that pales in comparison to the estimated amounts of copper we will need not only for renewable energies but also for construction, not only in China but throughout the world. But there is a better reason to use reserves in that they represent (in the vast majority of cases) the low-hanging fruit. The bulk of resources that are not marked as reserves are likely to be far beneath the earth's surface or found in dramatically reduced concentrations and therefore much more expensive to mine.

Even reserves themselves are becoming more expensive to mine. Gavin Mudd, an Australian engineer, noted in a paper presented in 2009 at the Canadian Metallurgical Society that copper grades are in general declining, which means that it is getting more expensive to mine copper. This is a statement that has been echoed by the world's largest copper producers, such as Freeport-McMoRan Copper & Gold. (This strongly suggests that we have reached, or are very close to, a copper peak, and it belies the current estimates of copper resources.) Mudd also notes, "It is well recognized that as ore grades decline energy-carbon costs increase, which will feedback in some manner to Cu [copper] prices."

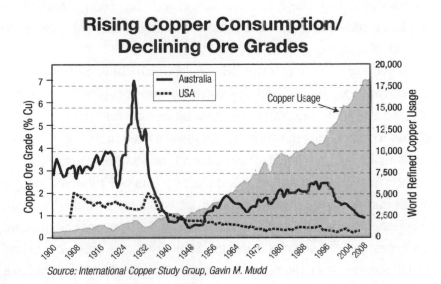

Rising Copper Consumption/ Declining Ore Grades

Source: International Copper Study Group, Gavin M. Mudd

Thus, as energy prices rise so does the cost of mining copper. As a result, both reserves and resources, which are calculated on today's energy prices, may be overstated, with resources likely to be overstated by a great deal. That is because the amount of energy needed to extract copper from ever poorer ore grades often sharply accelerates.

Rising Demand for Finite Resources

Now let's turn to China and its prospective need for copper. According to *Technology Review*, the country plans to spend $300 billion on copper for high-voltage power lines that will be necessary for constructing its electric grid. So just for its electric grid China will need almost 10 percent of the copper that is left in the ground worldwide. That's exclusive of other uses of copper, such as for housing and transportation, and, of course, power grids in other developing countries such as India, not to mention the large amount of copper the United States will require to construct our own smart grid.

Also consider the amount of energy and other resources (including copper itself) necessary to mine copper. Building machines, building infrastructure as in Afghanistan, feeding workers, and virtually all activities associated with the metal's extraction will take energy. And as we mentioned above, as copper gets scarcer the amount of energy needed to mine it will increase.

Then there is the automotive industry, of which China has become the largest player. Right now there are about a billion cars plying the world's roads. One major worldwide goal is to transition from internal combustion engines to hybrid cars in which batteries play a major role. Suppose your goal is half a billion hybrids. That might not be so unreasonable just for China, which currently only has around fifty cars per thousand people and is offering major incentives to buy hybrids. But what would that mean for copper? Hybrid cars require about twice as much copper as standard cars because of the vehicles' batteries. Some estimates are that a hybrid car will require about 100 pounds of copper. Just simple math shows that we will need about 23 million tons of copper—almost 5 percent of total copper reserves—if that half a billion cars target is to be met.

Keep in mind that copper is only one of several resource issues when it comes to cars. There is also the question of lithium, which is needed for the batteries most likely to power cars. Major portions of the world's deposits of lithium are located in politically and geologically challenging environments, such as Bolivia. According to Meridian Research International, lithium reserves could be exhausted in as few as twenty years once the manufacturing of hybrid and electric cars moves into the fast lane. And that would put a tremendous pressure on lithium recycling which is costly and difficult. (As of today, there is no recycling of lithium.)

There are electric motors under development that would not need batteries. One, the switched reluctance motor, has been around for twenty years, and though it is still not at the stage that it could be used to power an automobile, there is that possibility. But even this motor does not get around the scarcity of copper, which would be used extensively in the motor's dynamics. As we will show below, there is just no way to connect the dots between potential copper demand and copper supplies. Clearly the Chinese actions in both Africa (which we will get to shortly) and Afghanistan are evidence that they get it in spades, while we remain utterly complacent and completely in the dark.

As far as inflation is concerned, Mark Jacobson's assumptions are that economies of scale will likely compensate or more than compensate for any rise in commodity prices. This means, for example, that the more windmills we produce the cheaper it will be to produce them. But as we saw a few years ago, windmill prices rose as rising iron ore and other commodity prices overwhelmed the economies of scale.

While Jacobson does not completely ignore scarcity issues, he assumes that we will be able to deal with them. For instance, in the case of one of the most important rare earth elements, neodymium, he simply calculates the world's estimated reserves and potential production from those reserves. He ignores the fact that these reserves are highly toxic to produce, mostly located in one country, China, and will themselves require increasing amounts of resources to produce.

It is pretty clear from just this one example that the costs are going to be considerably higher than Jacobson estimates. Or, more specifically, the prorated costs for the developed world will be considerably higher. In the case of rare earths, China has a major cost edge, which we will discuss shortly, but here we want to focus on the big metals—especially copper, but also others such as iron ore and silver—that are assumed to be relatively plentiful and to offer no meaningful constraints. Indeed, in a 2009 article in a specialized energy journal, Jacobson discussed the problem of rare earth elements and noted the following quote from a 2009 article in *Magnetics and Business Technology* by Tony Morcos, an expert in magnetic circuit design and analysis:

A possible dwindling of the permanent magnet supply caused by the wind turbine market will be self-limiting for the following reasons: large electric generators can employ a wide variety of magnetic circuit topologies, such as surface permanent magnet, interior permanent magnet, wound field, switched reluctance, induction and combinations of any of the above. All of these designs employ large amounts of iron (typically in the form of silicon steel) and copper wire, but not all require permanent magnets. Electric generator manufacturers will pursue parallel design and development paths to hedge against raw material pricing, with certain designs making the best economic sense depending upon the pricing of copper, steel and permanent magnets. Considering the recent volatility of sintered NdFeB [an acronym for a neodymium magnet] pricing, there will be a strong economic motivation to develop generator designs either avoiding permanent magnets or using ferrite magnets with much lower and more stable pricing than NdFeB.

In other words, there is no need to worry about rare earths because of abundant supplies of copper and iron. But that simply is not true, and when it comes to copper, it is completely false.

For starters, we already know that Jacobson is at odds with the Yale professors' 2006 analysis of several of these metals. But these professors were not even considering the role of renewable energies when they did their analysis. Factoring in renewable energies, virtually all major materials have become extremely scarce—and will become even more so, perhaps at an exponential rate, as we go forward. Let's be a bit more precise about China and copper. Over the past several years China's consumption has been growing at a rate well in excess of 10 percent—and this period included the recession-torn 2009 in which even China's growth dipped to about 6 percent. Copper is the one significant commodity whose growth rate has exceeded the growth in the economy. The reason is that copper is at the sweet spot of the country's development, which has been centered on infrastructure, energy, and urbanization, all of which use a lot of the metal. Though the country wants to shift toward a more consumer-oriented society, that switch will require massive urbanization and construction. Then there is alternative energy. Just the amount of copper the country will need for high-voltage wires will add at least two percentage points to the growth in copper consumption. And of course there is the possibility that China has been stockpiling copper and will continue to do so.

Again, a little math shows some very chilling results. Suppose China's growth in copper consumption remains at around 11 percent until 2020; its usage of the metal by then would be over 17 million tons per year, which would be about 8 percent more than all the copper produced in 2009! Before you say that such a growth assumption is just too high, consider again that China has only begun to build out its renewable energy program, its urbanization efforts are perhaps only 30 or 40 percent complete, and that even greater stockpiles will have to be accumulated for the ten years following 2020. Our assumptions are that China's alternative energies will only account for about 16 percent of total energy consumption by the end of this decade. Moreover, even at a 9 percent rate of growth in copper consumption—more than 20 percent less than recent growth rates—China by 2020 would be consuming almost as much copper as the entire world is today.

Then there are also comparisons with other countries that have gone through developmental stages. For example, Japan at its peak consumption of copper was consuming about 14 kilograms per capita annually. In 2009 China's per capita consumption was about 4.6 kilograms per capita. To match Japan's per capita consumption, China's will have to triple. Yet alternative energies were a small part of Japan's copper consumption. Also true is that China's population is likely to grow in the decades ahead. And,

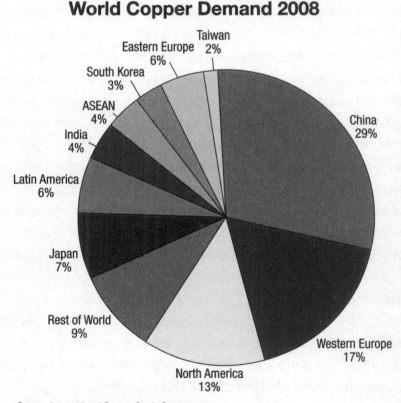

World Copper Demand 2008

Taiwan 2%
Eastern Europe 6%
South Korea 3%
ASEAN 4%
India 4%
Latin America 6%
Japan 7%
Rest of World 9%
North America 13%
Western Europe 17%
China 29%

Source: International Copper Study Group

of course, remember the relative sizes of the countries. Wiring a larger country will likely require even more copper per capita.

The bottom line is that a tripling of Chinese copper consumption by 2020 would still leave its per capita consumption less than Japan's at its peak.

Keep in mind that the game does not end in 2020; it ends because of ultimate resource constraints. It is reasonable to project double-digit growth in China's copper consumption not only well into the decade but beyond. If you want to go beyond 2020 the results become even more chilling. For example, were China's copper consumption to grow at an 8.5 percent rate over the next twenty years, the total amount of copper the country would consume would amount to about 60 percent of the world's reserves. No matter how you slice it, if China is going to build out renewable energies, no other country—including America—will be able to follow.

Why Substitution Just Won't Work

There are substitutes for copper, of course, such as aluminum. But assuming aluminum will fill the gap when copper isn't available is almost like a dog chasing its tail. The reason is that it takes tremendous amounts of energy and water to refine aluminum. If fossil fuels were not scarce, aluminum would be a substitute for copper in many applications—albeit a far from perfect one. (Aluminum pales in comparison to copper as both a thermal and an electric conductor, for instance.) But the biggest difference is that aluminum requires tremendous amounts of energy to refine. Ironically there are, for all practical purposes, almost unlimited amounts of the raw material, bauxite, required to make aluminum. But as we have explained, there is a rapidly growing shortage of the energy it takes to turn the bauxite into aluminum.

Between mid-2005 and mid-2010, copper traded at about three times the price of aluminum on a pound-for-pound basis, which reflects the fact that copper is a much more useful and versatile metal. Though there were days during the period in which the ratio was as high as five or six to one, substitution usually begins when the ratio exceeds three to one for a sustained period. Roughly speaking, this means that you need more than three pounds of aluminum to replace a pound of copper. At the same time, it takes about three times as much energy to produce a pound of aluminum versus a pound of copper. So substituting aluminum for copper will require nine times as much energy per unit of substitution. That is a lot. Suppose copper demand grows by a modest 3 percent a year over the next decade and the world attempts to substitute about a third of that copper with aluminum. The amount of energy it would take to refine the extra aluminum would be equivalent to the energy the entire world uses in seven to ten days.

There is no evidence that America has given even a moment's thought as to where all that extra energy is going to come from. The Chinese, by contrast, continue to accumulate every scrap of copper they can find, continue to mine copper in the world's most dangerous places, and continue to give every indication that they get it and get it in spades.

Interestingly, though they're scouring the planet for copper, their internal production of the metal is currently just 3 percent of the country's domestic reserves. For gold they're mining 16 percent of their reserves annually, for silver and zinc around 10 percent. Something just doesn't add up with copper. This suggests that either their reserves are of increasingly marginal quality, or they're just not there.

We have mentioned that the Chinese cherish virtually anything that contains even scraps of copper, silver, and other metals. It's estimated that a ton of discarded electronics can contain 1,000 parts per million (ppm) of gold, 2,000 ppm of silver, and 50 ppm of palladium, according to a study from the Norwegian University of Science and Technology. It is no wonder that every scrap of electronic waste is then a little treasure to the Chinese—even if that treasure is toxic and comes from America.

No one knows how much of these metals the Chinese have stockpiled, and conversations with miners and bureaucrats reaffirm that this kind of data is a state secret. But it is certain that stockpiles of everything from rare earths to copper to silver are as large as they can be without throwing the various markets out of balance.

Iron in the Line of Fire

Copper is clearly the metal whose scarcity we view as the most serious threat to worldwide development of new energies, but that does not mean we should overlook others. Iron ore is another metal we take for granted while the Chinese seemingly continue to accumulate almost all of it that they can purchase.

That's not surprising. The problem of scale and its impact on resource scarcity will affect even the most common of materials, including iron ore, the most readily available commodity that would be used in making wind turbines. Iron is one of the most common minerals in the earth's crust. Combined with nickel and other metals, it is the major component of steel. Among all the major raw materials on the planet, iron is putatively the one the world is least likely to run short of. But let's look a little closer.

Today, there are three major iron ore–exporting nations: India, Australia, and Brazil. Together they provide 70 percent of the world's exports

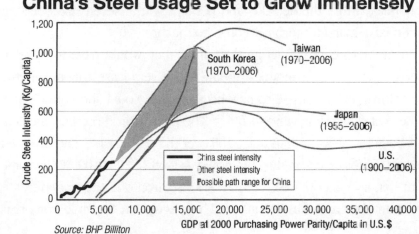

China's Steel Usage Set to Grow Immensely

Source: BHP Billiton

of iron. Not surprisingly, China is the world's largest iron consumer and importer. Apart from these three exporters, most countries that produce iron ore use it entirely to satisfy domestic demand. They have no excess ore available to export. In fact, India has been hinting recently that it may need to stop exporting iron because its own consumption has been rising faster than production. That would leave the world with just two iron exporters in the fairly near future.

The iron market is expected to grow by 4 to 5 percent annually during the next several years to support the construction taking place in the developing world and elsewhere. We think there is real question as to whether Australia and Brazil will be able to meet that demand under current conditions. Then there are windmills—millions of them—not included in current calculations. If those windmills were constructed over a twenty-year period it would add about 20 percent to the amount of iron ore the world would need.

For one thing, though Brazil's and Australia's reserve base is a small fraction of the world's total iron ore reserves, the pair are particularly rich in iron and have considerable infrastructure in place that allows the iron to be transported to the desired markets. If we conservatively assume their currently stated reserves are accurate, and apply standard geological analysis, Brazil's and Australia's iron production from existing reserves will likely peak within the decade—and perhaps within seven years or so if additional demand for turbines comes to the fore.

In order to continue to produce iron, they would have to develop reserves that are uneconomical today. At the very least, this means the price of iron ore must rise to new heights. This would add considerably to the cost of building wind turbines. The price of iron ore has, incidentally, been rising faster than that of oil over the past decade, and dropped far less than oil prices in the commodity sell-off of 2008–09. While some claim that speculators were behind oil's rise, iron ore isn't traded in the futures markets and thus isn't affected by speculation. So while iron ore is one of the most plentiful elements on earth, we question just how plentiful it is in view of the world's future needs.

There's no guarantee that enough new deposits could be developed fast enough to prevent wind turbines from becoming cost-prohibitive. With India out of the picture, the world would have to turn to places like the former Soviet Union, such as Russia and Ukraine. But frankly, we doubt these countries could deliver enough iron to meet the world's demand. For one thing, they would have to spend massive amounts of energy and resources (including steel) in order to build the infrastructure to produce iron ore. Delivery would also be a problem. Building just one 5-megawatt turbine takes over 1,000 tons of steel. Multiply that by the 3.8 million turbines our friend Mark Jacobson of Stanford University believes will be required as part of a proposal to meet 100 percent of the world's energy needs via a combination of renewable energy sources and you get some idea why nearly preternatural infrastructure and transportation costs are associated with the development of iron ore deposits.

Just to produce the extra steel—assuming there is enough iron ore available—would require the amount of energy the world currently uses in about twenty days. And that's a very conservative estimate. For China to achieve its own renewable goal by 2020 by using wind alone would mean about 33 percent of its electricity would come from wind, which would be equivalent to an extra day of global energy production and would add about 10 percent to the world's steel production.

Perhaps the strongest evidence that steel and energy are closely linked is the very strong relationship between energy—and in particular oil—prices and iron ore prices. As we mentioned above, in 2008 when oil was making spectacular highs, so was iron ore. More recently, iron ore prices—perhaps because the metal is lot more scarce than most realize— have been outperforming oil prices. An additional 10 percent of iron ore production would likely be a nearly impossible pill for America to swallow in terms of the added cost of iron ore. Chinese stockpiles not only give them an insurmountable edge but assure ever greater taxes on American consumers in the form of burgeoning commodity prices.

No Silver Lining

Like copper, silver is vital for the development of a low-carbon economy run primarily on renewable energy. *And supplies of silver are likely to fall far short of the world's needs in just a few short years, though hardly anyone is aware of this danger.*

Silver is regarded as a precious metal and has been used as money for about five thousand years. But silver is much more than a decoration or a coin; it is also an industrial metal with some very special properties that make it nearly essential in all sorts of electronic devices and also in most applications of solar energy.

Silver's critical role in common types of solar modules comes from the fact that the metal is the best thermal and electric conductor in the world. Estimates are that it takes between 50 and 125 tons of silver to produce one gigawatt of solar power. As of 2009, less than 23 gigawatts of solar power had been installed worldwide. But solar power has been growing by around 37 percent a year since 2000, with the rate lately accelerating. And nowhere has it grown faster than in China.

Since 2003, solar energy manufacturing has been growing by well over 100 percent a year in China, though the vast majority of these solar modules are exported. Much as the Pentagon acted as the primary market for the U.S. semiconductor industry in its infancy in the 1960s and 1970s while those manufacturers gained economies of scale, China is exporting solar panels to America and other nations, using its competitive advantages in labor, land, and taxes to dominate the market. There may come a day before long when China retains its solar production for itself, or at least greatly reduces the number of solar modules available for export, much as it has with rare earth elements. The only thing preventing the country from doing this so far is its lack of a smart grid with which to effectively manage the flow of power, a situation it is working hard to rectify in a few short years. Having ceded the solar business to the Chinese, we will be ill-prepared to fill the demand gap when that fateful day occurs. Moreover, even before that day arrives nature may put the brakes on the development of wide-scale solar power adoption.

Future growth in solar power capacity is likely to be severely constrained, as silver supplies are sharply limited. Some 22,000 tons of silver are mined each year, while only around 510,000 tons are considered to be economically viable reserves. This makes silver one of the world's most economically scarce metals.

Silver output is largely derived as a by-product of mining other metals. Less than a third of the metal mined each year comes from primary silver mines. It's more frequently found in conjunction with lead/zinc, copper, and gold deposits. Interestingly, despite sharp demand for those other metals and rising prices for silver in the twenty-first century, from a little more than $4 an ounce to more than $40, the supply of newly mined silver failed to rise meaningfully.

Industrial uses for silver, from water purification to electronic conductors, will consume about 70 percent of annual production within ten years. A big chunk of silver will also be used for investment and, of course, jewelry. Even if you assume efficiency gains in producing solar cells, silver will become in exceptionally short supply.

Let's suppose the Chinese understand this. As we said, the country has a stated goal of renewables generating 15 to 20 percent of its primary energy by 2020. Let's now assume that China delivers on its plan to become more energy-efficient and that energy use grows by just 4 percent a year between 2009 and 2020 (though even 4.5 percent energy growth would be low if the country's overall economic growth remains around 9 percent, which is very likely). That will mean that by 2020 the country will need about 4.5 terawatts (4.5 trillion watts) of capacity. Its goal is that about 16 percent of that capacity be renewable energies, or roughly 720 gigawatts.

Right now the projected goals of individual sources of renewable energies do not add up. Let's assume the country uses all its hydro capacity (about 300 GW), builds all the nuclear power plants it has planned (about 70 GW), uses about all its available biomass capacity (about 30 GW), and achieves its stated goals for solar (about 30 GW) and wind (about 100 GW). Those numbers add up to about 530 GW, which is nearly 200 GW short of the country's implied 2020 goal of about 720 GW. The only places that power can come from are wind and solar, as other sources are maxed out. (And, indeed, going past 2020, the only energy source you can add to the mix would be nuclear, as both bio- and hydropower would be maxed out by 2020 under our assumptions.)

If you tried to make up the 2020 shortfall with solar energy it would mean as much as an extra 20,000 tons of silver, which would be 20 percent of all mined and recycled silver that was not used for other industries. That is a big chunk and by itself likely enough to drive the silver market into severe deficits. Furthermore, even if the Chinese split the difference between wind and solar you would still likely see the silver market in a major deficit position. Also bear in mind that even 200 GW of solar would only be 28 percent of China's renewable goal by 2020.

It is clear that China can only rely on solar energy to a fairly limited extent. If it tried to replace 28 percent of its primary energy consumption with solar, it would consume about 20 percent of the world's current silver reserves. This kind of consumption precludes other countries, including the United States, from turning to solar energy to any meaningful extent unless we act immediately and start stockpiling massive amounts of silver. Even if new technologies reduce the amount of silver needed in solar cells, it won't help enough in that silver (and tremendous amounts of copper) will also be needed for the transmission of energy, which we do not count in our solar calculations. China's big head start in manufacturing solar panels along with the likelihood of their massive and growing stockpiles of the white metal clearly poses an enormous challenge to us.

As we move toward and past 2020 it's evident that any combination of solar and wind will assure dramatically higher commodity prices and major shortages of copper, silver, and even iron ore in addition to other less common metals. The most important implication is that these shortages will leave us unable to create renewable energies on our own. And we are only talking about what the Chinese are planning for the next decade. It goes without saying that as we go further into the future the situation will become worse—very likely catastrophically worse.

Chapter 5

Rare Earth Elements Are Getting Rarer— and China Has Them

There's a common assumption that if oil prices get too high, we will simply switch to using electric vehicles. Another prevalent supposition is that wind and solar power will soon light our houses and power our factories as we abandon coal-burning plants to combat global warming. This abiding faith that something better will come along (in a timely fashion no less) to replace what we've come to take for granted rests on an imprudent belief that technology *always* saves the day. But America will soon learn that this unswerving conviction is akin to driving along a twisting mountain road on a rainy night with no headlights or wipers to aid us.

Consider that we have yet to get started on assembling the infrastructure needed for the switch from gasoline-powered cars to plug-in hybrids and electric vehicles. Getting to the point where that network is widely installed will take time and money, both of which are in short supply. That's not to say this task is impossible, so suppose we do eventually get set up with ubiquitous rapid charging stations, leading to the widespread adoption of electric vehicles. There are certain key minerals known as rare earth elements (REEs), essential in the construction of electric motors and hybrid batteries, that the world does not have enough of, and for which there are no substitutes. Without them, rush hour on the streets and highways in our future will be crowded with bicycles rather than automobiles. In many respects our world will become a more local-centric place.

The bottom line is that rare earth elements are indispensable in the production of wind turbines and solar panels. Without them, the idea of moving our electrical production to alternative energy from the mere footnote that it is today to a significant contributor to our power requirements is a pipe dream.

On a personal level, we've grown accustomed to falling prices for electronics. Each successive product generation has become more powerful and less expensive than the last. But falling prices will not be a permanent fixture, whether it's for cell phones, laptops, or flat-panel TVs, given that there's a growing shortfall in the production of rare earth minerals used to manufacture these goods. On the contrary, as controversial as this sounds, many gadgets that are ever present today could soon be on their way to becoming luxury items.

Even the U.S. armed forces' commanding superiority in weapons systems could soon be compromised in important areas owing to a lack of these crucial materials. And without battlefield superiority, our service personnel will be ever more in harm's way.

This is not to say we're doomed. But if we're to have a chance at maintaining any semblance of the standard of living we take for granted, we must act soon and forcefully in building out a new energy economy, or we may never get the chance. As we'll show below, China already has a major hand in these developments coming to pass.

China's Stranglehold

Like anything else in this world, renewable energies are not free. Not free in any sense: Not only do they cost a lot of money to harness, but even more relevant, they require a lot of resources as well. In *Game Over* we wrote about the relationships among materials. We showed how virtually all materials share an interdependency with one another and have a direct impact on the development of alternative energies.

There's no way of building alternative energies without massive amounts of resources—including immense amounts of fossil fuels. But in addition to the well-known commodities such as oil, coal, water copper, iron ore, and the like, there are also lesser-known resources required for alternative energies, among them rare earth elements.

Though not needed in quantity, these materials are vital to building out both wind and solar systems, as well as hybrid and electric vehicles and a host of other high-tech applications including iPods, liquid crystal displays, catalytic converters, fiber optic cable, magnetic resonance

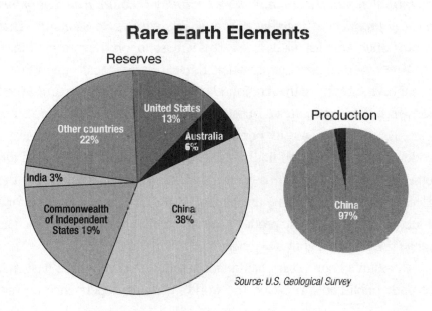

Rare Earth Elements

Reserves

United States 13%
Other countries 22%
Australia 6%
India 3%
Commonwealth of Independent States 19%
China 38%

Production

China 97%

Source: U.S. Geological Survey

imaging systems, and, most important, defense systems. This latter category includes precision-guided munitions, targeting lasers, avionics, radar systems, night vision equipment, satellites, and communications systems.

Before focusing on the better-known commodities we want to concentrate on these "weak links," for most of which America is wholly dependent on China—resources that could disappear altogether in just a few short years.

The seventeen minerals that comprise the so-called rare earth elements are really not that rare in that they can be found throughout the earth's crust. But they are rare in a couple of very important senses. There are few deposits that are large enough to mine in commercial quantities. Think of toy marbles. There may be a lot of them in the world, but if you want them in quantity it would be an expensive proposition going around to all the kids (and some grown-ups) who use them for recreational purposes.

The other difficulty associated with rare earths is that mining and refining them is highly polluting. For this reason most of the world's rare earth mines have been shuttered for a decade or more. *Indeed, the only country that mines these minerals in quantity is China, which as of this writing produces 97 percent of the world's rare earth elements.* That means when America needs rare earths it must import them from China.

We want to emphasize that not all rare earths are equally important—some have substitutes that are found in abundance. But there are several for which there are no ready substitutes. One is neodymium, a necessary ingredient in high-intensity permanent magnets. These magnets have a wide variety of uses, including an essential role in the motors of wind turbines. Without neodymium a wind turbine is much less efficient and the electricity that it generates is much more costly. The same can be said for a wide variety of electronic products, including military equipment such as range finders and night vision goggles.

Germany's Fraunhofer Institute for Systems and Innovation Research recently published a book on the world's growing dependence on raw materials for emerging technologies. To take just one example of how dire the situation is, consider that the institute concluded that by 2030 the world will need 3.8 times our current production of neodymium for applications such as permanent magnets and laser technology. Yet these applications already use up more than half the annual production of neodymium. Neodymium is a big deal and we import virtually every ounce we use from China.

Another example is europium, which is used to make fiber optics, lasers, and LED-based lights, which are energy-efficient replacements for both incandescent and compact fluorescent bulbs. Cerium is yet another; it and other rare earths are used as fluid-cracking catalysts, boosting yields and reducing the energy required to refine petroleum.

Given the severity of the situation, one would think that the United States would be taking action to ensure its supply of these increasingly vital resources. On the contrary: The country has ceased REE production and has gone from being self-sufficient to relying completely on imports.

It is instructive to see how we got into this position. In the 1980s we did mine rare earths in America. It was then that China began to sell rare earths at prices well below the costs of our mines. China not only had the advantage of cheap labor but also a cavalier attitude toward pollution. The largest mine in the United States—Molycorp's Mountain Pass in California's upper Mojave Desert—was the dominant source for our REE needs until production was shut down in the mid-1980s along with that of other mines around the world. Once a mine is shuttered for a long period it's not easy to reopen. Molycorp has been refining and selling REE from its stockpiled reserves since it ceased mining. Given the severity of the forecasted shortage, the company hopes to restart mining by 2012, but full-scale operations may be farther off.

According to a rare earth mining consultant, who was quoted in the May 4, 2010, *Science* magazine, "New mining efforts are just the first step. Numerous rare earth oxides are invariably mixed together in ores. They must be separated and purified, reduced to metallic form, and then alloyed, cast, and shaped. All the Western businesses that used to do these jobs are gone and will need to be restarted. Setting up this full suite can cost hundreds of millions of dollars and take up to a decade to accomplish." The article goes on to say that one of the only ways the mine will be reopened is if the U.S. government will be willing to bankroll loans worth $2 billion. Its reason to do this would be the essential nature of rare earths for critical military equipment.

Another way would be for automakers, anxious to segue to greener technologies, to offer to pay for the mining and refining of rare earths. Toyota recently initiated a venture with a Vietnam-based miner to secure supplies of neodymium and lanthanum, another rare earth element. Both are essential in the building of electric cars. A Prius car motor contains 2.2 pounds of neodymium, and each battery has more than 22 pounds of lanthanum. A 3-megawatt wind turbine, incidentally, contains roughly two tons of rare earths. Of course, the point that stands out is that rare earths have critical roles in a variety of green technologies.

Whether it be wind turbines or electric cars (or even vital military equipment and various electronic devices), rare earth elements are necessary. Moreover, despite more than a generation of efforts to replace the special properties that neodymium and other rare earths impart, material scientists have come up empty. (There is an argument that technology, as if it is some deity, will solve our problems. These arguments go by the wayside when it has been twenty-five years since the Nobel Prize was awarded to the creators of high-temperature superconducting materials. Remember then the promise of room-temperature superconductivity—a breakthrough that would have solved most of our energy problems? That promise is still just a dream, with absolutely no path to fulfilling it.)

How has China come to utterly dominate the production of these critical elements? By being ruthless in how it priced these products. In countries where free enterprise rules, the motivation for producing something is profits. If there are no profits, a project won't be initiated. So for a major mining project to be launched in America its owners have to be convinced the price of the metal or element will be high enough over the long term not only to cover the costs of creating the mine but also to produce a profit after all initial start-up and operating costs. In other words, the company has to have great confidence in the long-term prospects for what it is mining.

But in a country governed by state capitalism the rules are different. For one thing, the calculus in looking at the future does not have to be determined by a company's profit and loss statement, but rather by what is in the best long-term interest of the state. Obviously China calculated long ago that it was in its interest to control REEs. In 1992, in fact, Chinese leader Deng Xiaoping made his now famous proclamation, "There is oil in the Middle East; in China there is rare earths." Rather than using their cost advantages to create a profitable industry, the Chinese were willing to forsake profits so that no one else could compete. And they have not since changed their stripes.

In 2009 America paid about $85 million for its imports of REEs. Now, reflect a second before you conclude that the Chinese were just being magnanimous and granting us a massive discount on what is clearly a crucial material. If the market for a product is $85 million, are you as an investor going to put billions of dollars into a mine in which your total revenues are less than $100 million? Not unless you have lost your mind. And that is exactly why when it comes to reopening mines like Molycorp's Mountain Pass, loan and purchase guarantees from governments and other parties become necessary. In America and other developed countries, these kinds of guarantees take time, sometimes months, often years. Even if Congress immediately authorized the appropriate loan or purchase agreements, there could still be big obstacles with environmental permits. Indeed, given the toxic nature of this mining, there almost surely would be such problems.

How much of a lead does China have on the United States and other countries? It is surely measured in years, not months. Following a mid-2010 public offering to raise funds to reopen its mine, Molycorp will require more than a year to refurbish the operation and even longer to process its output. And the most it will be able to produce is about 10 percent of the world's supply of REEs. So under the best-case scenario China still has the upper hand—in a big way—in these utterly critical commodities.

The Chinese have taken aggressive actions to ensure their stockpiles and supply chain of REEs to meet their future domestic needs. Their Ministry of Industry and Information Technology (MIIT) has announced that it will create a reserve for rare earth metals beginning in 2011. But this is only the latest step. China instituted an export quota in 1998 and since 2005 has forced a downward trend on exports, with an average yearly decrease of 10 percent. In 2009 the country exported less than half of the rare earths it mined. According to the draft *Rare Earths Industry Development Plan 2009–2015* report from MIIT, the country will place a total ban on exports of the heavy rare earth elements dysprosium, lutetium, terbium, thulium, and yttrium within the next several years; exports of neodymium, europium, cerium, and lanthanum will be restricted to a combined quota of around 15,000 tons a year, down from 38,189 tons in 2008 and 48,040 tons in 2004. That's far below the world's current requirements, and it threatens to stymie the development of a wide range of emerging technologies, including superconductors, high-flux magnets, and refining catalysts. Hybrid and electric cars and wind power generation are just a few technologies that will be impacted by higher rare earth prices.

Protests against China's restricting the flow of rare earth exports have been met with the argument that the country's actions are intended to minimize pollution. While there may be an element of truth in that China wants to halt REE production by small-time operations that are difficult to supervise, it shows no signs that it is reducing production of these minerals. So while the Chinese appear to be taking the moral high ground, limiting rare earth exports as fighting pollution, they are actually hiding their resource accumulation under the guise of climate concerns, which is disingenuous. In addition to constricting REE outflow, state-owned companies have made multiple strategic acquisitions outside of China to solidify the nation's dominance of the market. The Chinese would own Molycorp today if CNOOC, the China National Offshore Oil Corporation, had succeeded in its bid to acquire Unocal in 2005. The California-based oil company owned the rare earth miner at the time and avoided being swallowed by the Chinese giant only because of congressional opposition to the deal on national security grounds. Instead, Unocal was acquired by Chevron, which later sold Molycorp to a group of private investors

Japan and the United States are considering taking the rare earth export issue to the World Trade Organization, but it remains to be seen if they'll succeed in forcing China to relinquish more of these important minerals. China can always argue that rare earths aren't so rare and that the United States and other countries have the ability to produce them should they choose to do so. As a fallback, China could also declare rare earths to be "strategic minerals," much the way Chile has with lithium, thereby regulating all sales of the elements and retaining them entirely for domestic use.

Keep in mind that unlike the 1973–74 Arab oil embargo, China isn't necessarily trying to hold anyone hostage by limiting rare earth supplies. Instead, it sees these elements as imperative to its own development, as early in the coming decade the country's own consumption of the rare earths is likely to exceed its production. In the meantime, though, China has used its REE dominance as a lever to induce foreign companies to set up shop on its soil. A number of U.S., Japanese, and European technology vendors have moved operations there to ensure access to REEs in the face of export controls.

All Solar Energy Goes Through China

Rare earth elements are but one of many examples that convincingly show that China's alternative energies and energy security trump virtually any other economic goal it expresses. The toxic nature of REEs and China's willingness to cut corners in its mining belie its passion about pollution and global warming.

One other material most people have probably not heard of that also merits a mention is indium. It is rarer than rare earths but still not one of the scarcest metals on the planet. By some estimates it is about three times more common in the earth's soil than silver. But relative abundance does not tell the whole story. The reason is that indium is not found in an isolated state. It must be refined from other metals—mostly zinc. Setting up refining operations is not an easy task, as evidenced by the fact that there are no indium refining operations in the United States. And that means that, as with rare earth elements, we import 100 percent of our indium needs. That's not a comfortable position, for this metal has special properties that cannot—at least based on present knowledge—be duplicated.

Indium is necessary for making flat-screen TVs and sundry consumer electronic devices, but what's really significant is that, along with silver, it's critical for creating solar energy. The broad-based adoption of solar energy is unlikely to happen without indium. Silver can be a substitute, but as we have shown, it too is scarce. Furthermore, in some applications— especially thin film solar—indium is essential. Since the vast majority of indium comes from zinc, the two necessities for producing indium are an adequate zinc supply and the ability to refine indium from it.

In 1999 the United States imported about 30 percent of our zinc and all our indium. The reason for our reliance on imports was summed up in the Commodity Research Bureau's *CRB Commodity Year Book 2000*: "The indium market appeared to be approaching long-term price stability, with increases in demand met by adequate supply and greater efficiency in processing." The last indium held by the U.S. government stockpile was sold in December 1998. In 1999 indium prices were less than $100 per pound. Today they are more than $400 per pound. And to the extent that solar energy becomes a substitute for fossil fuels, indium prices are headed "to the sun." Yet we still do not refine indium in this country. And when it comes to zinc our reliance on imports has grown from about 30 percent in 1999 to about 75 percent today.

Now contrast that with what has been going on in China. In 1999 China and the United States produced about the same amount of zinc, though in contrast to the United States, China did refine indium from their zinc and accounted for about 20 percent of the world's supply. Fast-forward two decades to today. U.S. production of zinc has declined and China now produces more than four times what the United States mines—and more than twice as much as the second largest producer. China alone accounts for 50 percent of the world's indium supply today. Two other Asian countries, South Korea and Japan, together account for another 25 percent or so.

The bottom line is that if the United States ever gets serious about solar energy, all roads must go through China. That's potentially disastrous. For recently China has indicated that as with rare earths, it's planning to cut back on its exports of the metal. Attempting to guess how long it would take the United States to get up to speed in acquiring enough indium to satisfy our future needs, either through exports from sources other than China or our own devices, is a nearly hopeless task. But we suspect a decade or more would be a conservative estimate.

Likewise, in 2010, the U.S. General Accountability Office, citing industry estimates, forecast that rebuilding a U.S. rare earth supply chain may take up to fifteen years and is dependent on several factors, including securing capital investments for infrastructure, developing new technologies, and acquiring patents, which are currently held by international companies.

This chapter, as with so many in this book, is tough to sum up because its conclusions are so grim. As we showed in chapter 3, it's clear that the United States can no longer assume that fossil fuels are available for the taking. Their growing scarcity has been a major reason that the 2000s were one of the worst decades for Americans economically. And this scarcity will only grow. Without other sources of energy, which require scarce minerals, our lifestyles will continue to decline—perhaps exponentially.

Rising costs will leave less income available for anything beyond life's essentials. The service sector, by far the largest segment of our economy today, will likely contract substantially. As a result, if we stay on our present course millions of American jobs will disappear, creating a host of social ills.

We need new energy sources in the worst way to offset this expected decline. That means renewable energies are going to have to play an increasing role. The two most scalable renewables are wind and solar. Yet we lack the materials to scale up in either one. These essential materials are either monopolized or controlled by the Chinese. Unfortunately, it won't get better as you continue to read.

Chapter 6

Other Critical Commodities and China's Global Land Grab

Americans have been wearing blinders for the past decade. Our declining economy should have been enough to convince us that unless we become less reliant on critical materials, our lifestyles are destined to fall at an ever faster rate. Indeed, even America's most important source of strength—our vast military establishment—could end up seriously threatened by a massive shortage of a wide range of critical materials. A weakened military would then become part of a vicious circle in which America becomes ever weaker. Remember, the country that controls the vast majority of these materials is China.

While we continue to stress that China's aims are not to destroy the United States, we also can't emphasize enough that the battle for materials in which China is winning (by what could already be an insurmountable margin) is a battle for our freedoms, for our way of life, for everything that is America. An America sharply weakened militarily and faced with acute shortages of daily necessities is an America that may lose many of its basic freedoms. Indeed, it is hard to imagine any major nation in this situation existing as a free and vibrant democracy.

Perhaps the strongest evidence that America refuses to face the realities of our situation can be seen with a simple table. The data is separated by a decade and show the amount of various commodities that we import from abroad. The first shows the United States' dependence on nonfuel minerals circa 1999. We imported more than half our needs for twenty-seven minerals at the time, and we were completely dependent on imports for twelve. Of those twenty-seven, China was the most important exporter of twelve. It was also the chief supplier for three of the twelve minerals for which we were entirely import-dependent.

Fast-forward a decade and you find that the number of minerals for which the United States imports more than half of its needs has climbed to thirty-eight. And the number for which we are 100 percent dependent on others has jumped to nineteen. Of the thirty-eight, China is still the major source of eleven, but of the nineteen for which we are wholly dependent on imports, China is the chief source of eight. *In a decade we have gone from being substantially dependent on China for three materials to eight.*

America is becoming ever more dependent on others for its material needs, and the country whose mineral wealth is most critical for us has become China. This turn of events must be seen as a cause for concern, and indeed should incite plans to find alternative sources from allies rather than our greatest rival. Clearly anyone looking at this data would conclude that we do not take China seriously as an economic threat.

The perils of China's growing dominance in the mineral area go much further than mere numbers. Not all minerals and metals are created equal.

Last chapter we focused on rare earths and indium, probably the two most important materials for which we depend on China. In this chapter we take a more complete look at other materials for which China is our

U.S. Net Import Reliance on Selected Minerals

1999			2009		
Commodity	Imports	China's Role	Commodity	Imports	China's Role
Arsenic (trioxide)	100%	C*	Arsenic (trioxide)	100%	C*
Bauxite & Alumina	100		Asbestos	100	
Bismuth	100	C	Bauxite & Alumina	100	
Niobium	100		Cesium	100	
Fluorspar	100	C*	Fluorspar	100	C*
Graphite (natural)	100	C	Graphite (natural)	100	C*
Manganese	100		Indium	100	C*
Mica, sheet	100	C	Manganese	100	C
Strontium	100		Mica, sheet (natural)	100	C*
Thallium	100		Niobium	100	
Thorium	100		Quartz Crystal (industrial)	100	C*
Yttrium	100	C*	Rare Earths	100	C*
Gemstones	99		Rubidium	100	
Antimony	85	C*	Strontium	100	
Tin	85	C	Tantalum	100	C
Tungsten	81	C*	Thallium	100	
Chromium	80		Thorium	100	
Potash	80		Vanadium	100	
Tantalum	80	C	Yttrium	100	C*
Stone (dimension)	77		Gallium	99	C
Titanium (concentrates)	77		Gemstones	99	
Cobalt	73		Antimony	93	C*
Rare Earths	72	C*	Bismuth	90	C
Iodine	68		Germanium	90	C
Barite	67	C*	Platinum	89	
Nickel	63		Barite	80	C*
Peat	57		Tin	80	C
			Rhenium	79	
			Diamond (natural industrial)	78	
			Stone (dimension)	78	C
			Zinc	76	
			Cobalt	75	C
			Potash	73	
			Titanium (concentrates)	73	
			Titanium (sponge)	67	C
			Silver	63	
			Tungsten	63	C*
			Peat	60	

	1999	2009
No. Import dependence = 100%:	12	19
No. Import dependence > 50%:	27	38

C* = China is the chief supplier; C = China is a primary supplier.
Note that the importance of certain minerals has changed over time.

Source: U.S. Geological Survey

primary source. In a 2010 report the European Union ranked fourteen materials as being both supply-constrained and having critical economic importance. Of these fourteen, China is the key provider to both Europe and the United States of eight, which are antimony, fluorspar, gallium, graphite, germanium, indium, rare earths, and tungsten.

In short, without ready access to these materials, production of a wide range of important goods is threatened, everything from semiconductor manufacturing and the production of small arms (antimony and gallium), to energy storage (fluorspar and graphite), to the production of both solar and wind energy (rare earths, indium, germanium, and gallium), to sophisticated military weapons (gallium, indium, rare earths, and antimony), to fiber optics (germanium).

In other words, without these materials we cannot maintain our economy and we will have no way to transition from an economy dependent on nonrenewable energies to one dependent on renewables.

Of course, some will argue that the way out of this mess is to duplicate the properties of the materials with our advanced technologies. But we cannot bet a lot on that happening. In many cases there are few if any substitutes for these minerals. And where substitutes can be used, the trade-offs can be prohibitive. As we'll discuss in chapter 8, America's complacency that advanced technology will save the day is misguided.

It would appear that the Chinese government recognizes all this. Rather than waiting around for a techno-miracle, it is rushing to lock up every available ounce of key materials it can get its hands on to build the foundations of an alternative energy economy while those essential materials are still available. All the while, America stands by casually watching, doing little to prepare for the gathering storm.

Out of Africa and In Comes China

In the nineteenth century, the likes of Henry Morton Stanley and Cecil Rhodes stalked across Africa to tap the continent's riches as European nations scrambled to lay claim to vast expanses of it. The colonial era has long since ended, yet a strong parallel can be drawn between that distant past and China's actions in Africa today.

China has become the world's greatest single source of low-cost manufactured goods. Producing these export goods and satisfying its own ever-growing needs requires immense quantities of raw materials. And it's going to need significantly more minerals if the country is to succeed in building out a full-scale alternative energy network. Nowhere is China's clamber to secure materials outside of its own borders greater than in Africa. But rather than marching in and seizing power through brute force, China comes with a blank checkbook and an army of construction workers eager to help build the trappings of a modern state. And Africans have welcomed them, giving the Chinese unfettered access to their land's immense mineral deposits in exchange.

The exact size of China's direct investment in Africa is unknown. It no longer makes that information public, nor is it available from African nations. It is clear, however, that China has surpassed the United States and France as Africa's largest trading partner. Remarkably, Sino-African trade grew to nearly $107 billion in 2008, up from just $10 billion in 2000, according to China's Ministry of Commerce. Chinese companies, running the gamut from giant state-owned enterprises to small-scale entrepreneurs and traders, are active in almost all sectors of the African economy. While China's activities in Africa and elsewhere are conducted by numerous entities, given the close ties between many of its larger private companies and the communist government, it's not unreasonable to think of them as a monolithic actor.

The growth in the relationship between China and Africa has given birth to the term "ChinAfrica," but China has long been no stranger to Africa. In the 1950s and 1960s it supplied fledgling African nations with financial aid and construction crews to help build railroads and highways in an effort to spread the socialist gospel and counterbalance Western influence. In the past decade, Chinese workers fanned out across Africa in great numbers—there are an estimated one million Chinese now residing across the continent—and Chinese aid money has flowed freely. This has been a direct outgrowth of China's *zou chuqu* policy, which translates to "go out." Since 2001 it has encouraged overseas activity by Chinese companies. As part of *zou chuqu*, in 2007 a fifty-year government fund was established to encourage Chinese companies to invest in Africa. But rather than descending on Africa for ideological reasons, they are now bent on exploiting the continent's untapped resources.

Most Westerners' perception of the size of Africa is greatly distorted by the Mercator projection used in many maps of the world, which artificially magnifies the size of land masses closer to the poles in order to fit the spherical globe onto a flat surface. In reality, the African continent is bigger than the United States, China, and all of Europe combined.

To that point, the surface of Africa has hardly been scratched, so to speak, in terms of exploiting the continent's mineral wealth. Within its boundaries are spectacular deposits of oil, coal, iron, zinc, lead, tungsten, cobalt, coltan, copper, molybdenum, manganese, chromium, antimony, niobium, industrial diamonds, uranium, platinum group metals, silver, and gold, as well as virtually every mineral important to our modern-day lives.

Yet despite its grand scale, Africa's collective gross domestic product is merely on par with that of Brazil. Eager to remedy this, and in many cases for their own personal aggrandizement, many African leaders are seeking to capitalize on the export of their nations' natural resources. Competition for these is open to all comers, but Western companies can't contend with what China is bringing to the table. It is literally changing the African landscape in a bid to lock up all its resources before other nations can.

According to the World Bank, China has structured infrastructure-for-resources deals with at least thirty-five Sub-Saharan countries. Chinese construction firms are building across Africa like gangbusters. Much of the Chinese money pouring in for infrastructure development is in the form of concessional loans, low-interest loans made in exchange for Chinese state-owned companies being granted access to resources. In addition to government guarantees for bank loans, Chinese firms receive export credits for financing the operational cost of African projects, as well as credits for capital goods and machinery. As a result of this support from the communist government, Chinese companies can provide infrastructure projects at a cost far below what their Western counterparts (who receive no such government subsidies) would have to spend.

But while the roads, railroads, and hydroelectric dams that make up the bulk of this aid are being built ostensibly for the benefit of the Africans, they serve the dual purpose of speeding the extraction and transportation of resources back to China, while generating revenue for companies in the Middle Kingdom, as most of the materials used in the construction are imported from China. This so-called aid actually does little to improve the employment situation in the target countries: Most of these infrastructure agreements stipulate that 70 percent of the contracted personnel working on the projects are Chinese. In many cases, Chinese firms are staffing these projects with former prisoners who have been offered reduced sentences in exchange for serving these overseas operations.

The largest of these projects to date is in the Democratic Republic of the Congo (DRC), which spans an area in Central Africa approximately a quarter of the size of the United States. Its population of more than 70 million subsists on less than a dollar a day, the aftermath of colonial rule, corrupt leadership as an independent nation, and civil strife that left an estimated 5.4 million dead between 1998 and 2004 from war-related violence, disease, and starvation. Yet within its boundaries the DRC contains vast untapped mineral wealth. The nation's resources are estimated to be worth between $25 trillion and $50 trillion.

In a $9 billion infrastructure-for-minerals deal, China is getting resources it needs to power its voracious economy, while the DRC has and will receive a plethora of infrastructure projects built by a consortium of state-owned Chinese companies. The projects include 2,400 miles of roads, 2,000 miles of railroads, 32 hospitals, 145 health centers, and two universities. The DRC is largely devoid of paved roads, and travel between many of its cities is only practical by air. Life expectancy is less than fifty-five years, infant mortality is one of the highest in the world, and a third of the population is illiterate. So the lure of China's spending is irresistible for the leaders of the DRC, as it is in every other underdeveloped African country China has approached with similar deals.

China, for its part, is getting a heck of a bargain in the DRC. For its $9 billion in construction spending and loans it will mine 10 million metric tons of copper and 600,000 metric tons of cobalt. Even after deducting the share of those resources that will go to Gecamines, the DRC's parastatal mining company partnered in the venture, the value of the deal to China is at a minimum in the tens of billions of dollars.

Similar deals elsewhere in Africa have reportedly been heavily influenced by corruption, with suitcases full of cash and funding for pet projects, such as the construction of a new presidential palace (in Sudan), soccer stadiums (in Zambia and Kenya), and fiber optic Internet cable (Uganda). American companies are forbidden by law from engaging in bribery under the Foreign Corrupt Practices Act, but for Chinese firms such financial inducements are just a part of the cost of doing business.

Lacking a colonial history and given their past support of independence movements, the Chinese are welcomed partners in Africa, whereas Westerners are likely to be viewed with a jaundiced eye. China's approach to doing business in the developing world is pragmatic in the extreme. Whereas Western development aid is frequently tied to improved human rights and democratic reform, China's policy is both apolitical and amoral. It is willing to work with any and all regimes, regardless of their status in the international community.

Theodore H. Moran, Marcus Wallenberg Chair at the School of Foreign Service at Georgetown University and author of *China's Strategy to Secure Natural Resources: Risks, Dangers, and Opportunities*, notes that China's actions also have implications for rogue states, authoritarian leadership, civil wars, corruption, deterioration of governance standards, and the environment. Such effects may make patterns of Chinese resource procurement objectionable, on grounds quite apart from the debate about possible "lockup," "tie-up," and "control" of access on the part of China and Chinese companies.

Not only does China buy roughly half of Sudan's oil, but it in turn supplies that government with the weapons to carry out genocide. Chinese arms are also a fixture in Zimbabwe, supporting the tyrannical Robert Mugabe in exchange for entrée into the country's diamond fields.

A miscellaneous provision in the financial reform bill President Obama signed into law in July 2010 to curb the excesses in the banking sector sought to address the issue of "conflict minerals." Specifically, the measure was aimed at stopping the traffic in minerals from the DRC. The law requires American companies to submit annual reports to the Securities and Exchange Commission disclosing whether their products contain tantalum, gold, tungsten, or other minerals sourced from the DRC or adjacent countries. There's no penalty for using minerals from these nations, but doing so would become a matter of public record.

While this law is a noble endeavor to deny funds to organizations that engage in violence—including systematic gang rape—and it may induce American companies to source their minerals from outside that conflict-torn region, Chinese manufacturers will continue to obtain minerals there. Indeed, they'll be happy to purchase what the Americans no longer buy.

As Jeffrey Sachs, professor of economics and director of the Earth Institute at Columbia University, phrased it, "China gives fewer lectures and more practical help." China's only stipulation in giving aid to a country is an insistence on the recipient's recognition of the "One China" principle—Beijing's objective of isolating Taiwan from the rest of the world. All this gives the Chinese a tremendous leg up when competing against American or European companies for access to materials.

As an aside, for all of their newfound environmental concerns at home, Chinese companies have demonstrated almost no regard for conservation in Africa, where enforcement is lax and the right officials can be easily bought off. Western companies don't always have the best record in this area either, but they are more apt to conform with local laws. Among the bodies that have raised concerns about China on this issue is the United Nations Conference on Trade and Development, which fears that the disregard of best environmental practices and China's policy of noninterference in domestic affairs tend to undermine governance standards observed under the OECD Convention on Combating Bribery. This disregard for the environment in Africa underscores that China is largely using climate change as a cover to obtain dwindling resources before the rest of the world wises up and pursues a similar path.

The list of resource deals China has struck is growing rapidly. Oil from Sudan, Angola, Nigeria, and Ghana; iron ore from Sierra Leone; manganese from Gabon; uranium from Zimbabwe; copper from Zambia and the DRC; timber from Madagascar—the list goes on. Our concern that China is seeking these long-term sources of resources not only to fuel its economy but to reshape it around renewable energy while the United States and its allies procrastinate is no mere hand-wringing. Even if the world is not in danger of running out of certain resources per se, the lack of availability, even if only temporary, could cause great upheaval for the United States and put our national security at risk.

Consider China's play for coltan. That's the popular term for columbite-tantalite, an ore from which tantalum is extracted. Though you've probably never heard of it, tantalum touches your life daily in many ways. It is primarily used for capacitors in electronic circuits, where it's prized for its ability to store and release an electric charge with minimal power loss. Cell phones and laptop computers, for instance, all contain tantalum, as do countless other electronic devices. Tantalum's physical properties, such as heat and chemical corrosion resistance, as well as its hardness and ductility, have led to its widespread use by the defense/aviation industry, where it is used to create superalloys for jet engines, among other things. It is also employed in medical equipment such as implants and joint replacement parts.

Sixty-four percent of the world's estimated reserves of coltan are in the DRC. Consumption of tantalum has grown at a steady 6 percent pace during the last two decades. If the entire world were to achieve a usage rate for tantalum of just half that of the United States it would exhaust available supply in a mere two decades. Only a handful of companies process tantalum. Three firms, U.S.-based Cabot Corporation, Germany's HC Starck, and China's state-owned Ningxia Non-ferrous Metals Smeltery, account for 80 percent of the mineral's demand Due to international pressure against the trafficking in "conflict minerals"—minerals mined in strife-torn regions—Cabot and HC Starck have pledged not to source their tantalum ore from the DRC. Ningxia, in contrast, either purchases up to half of its ore from the Central African nation directly or acquires ore smuggled out of the DRC and sold in neighboring countries. The United States is the second largest consumer of tantalum behind China, and we are increasingly dependent on the communist country to meet our needs for this important mineral.

Africa is the key source for many other indispensable minerals. Failure to secure adequate supplies of any one of a number of them could deal our nation a critical setback, from which we could have a difficult time recovering.

Cobalt is an essential mineral used in industrial and military applications, with limited substitutes available—most of which would lead to a drop in production performance The DRC is home to nearly half the world's cobalt reserves. The mineral can be found in the United States, but it has not been mined here since 1971, and much higher prices would be required to make such operations economical again. In the meantime, a disruption in American cobalt supplies could prove detrimental to our economy. China has become the world's leading producer of refined cobalt, though it imports much of its cobalt-rich ore from Congo.

Another mineral critical to the United States for which we are entirely dependent on imports is manganese. Manganese is essential in steel production, and there are no economical substitutes for it. Used in conjunction with aluminum, antimony, and copper, the hard but brittle metal can also be used to form ferromagnetic alloys. Manganese is seemingly in great supply, but its role in alternative energy could change that. For instance, the metal could potentially double the life of lithium-ion batteries, which would greatly increase demand for it.

Manganese is found in several parts of the world in deposits of other minerals, though never as a free metal on its own. More than 80 percent of known manganese resources are located in South Africa; another 10 percent are in Ukraine. It's also found in China and a handful of other countries, including Gabon, the source for about 60 percent of U.S. manganese ore imports. Nearly a fifth of America's ferromanganese now comes from China.

China's resource deals aren't just limited to Africa. In Southeast Asia, for instance, it has made concessional loans and is building hydroelectric dams (not to mention providing military hardware and diplomatic protection) for the military junta of Myanmar, a pariah on the international stage, in exchange for access to resources such as oil and nickel.

It has also been active across Latin America, setting up concessional loans in the tens of billions, and to a lesser degree investing in infrastructure, to lock up long-term supplies of resources. In one example, it has inked a deal with Venezuela, the largest oil producer in South America and the fourth largest supplier to the United States, which is shipping crude to China as a means of repaying $20 billion of debt the country borrowed to finance power, agriculture, and technology projects. As Venezuela ramps up its exports to a million barrels a day by 2012, it will leave less oil available for the United States to purchase.

China's deals in Latin America have largely centered on its gaining access to crude oil, but they also include deals for natural gas, iron ore, copper, and other minerals. In addition to Venezuela, China has signed notable agreements with Brazil, Bolivia, Ecuador, and Argentina.

China's aggressive actions in Africa and elsewhere to secure long-term supplies of increasingly scarce natural resources have implications well beyond what Americans pay for their gasoline, cell phones, and other electronic devices. In the long term, China's control of key resources from

Africa could make us hostage to our greatest adversary—a situation no American should be content to let stand.

U.S. Congress Asleep at the Wheel, Again

The U.S. military is aware of the likelihood of critical shortages of important minerals it needs for national defense, most of which come from foreign sources—including China—but it's hampered by a federal government that appears unconcerned with this state of affairs and which moves at a glacial pace.

In its preparations ahead of open conflict with Hitler's Germany, in 1939 the U.S. War Department established a strategic reserve of metals and minerals it would need for the war effort. This reserve was maintained throughout the cold war, and it survives today as the Defense National Stockpile Center (DNSC) at Fort Belvoir in northern Virginia.

The reserve still warehouses and manages the acquisition and disposition of limited supplies of critical minerals in depots throughout the United States. But in the wake of the collapse in the Soviet Union, in 1992 Congress directed the DNSC to sell the bulk of the commodities being held in the stockpile. The reserve was seen as a relic of the cold war that we no longer needed. Congress was also eager to reap the so-called "Peace Dividend," and this source of funds yielded $6.6 billion for the American government in the ensuing five years. At the time, the thinking was that these strategic minerals would remain abundantly available should the need for them ever arise. The stockpile, which at the end of the cold war held ninety different commodities stored in eighty-five locations, was reduced to just seventeen in three locations by the end of 2007.

In a 2008 study titled *Managing Materials for a Twenty-first Century Military*, the National Research Council (NRC) of the National Academies of Science addressed the need for a defense stockpile and came to a decidedly different conclusion. The study was conducted in light of the fact that our military-industrial complex has changed radically since the strategic reserve was initially established. The supply of defense systems, once dominated by the government, is now driven by civilian industry that increasingly depends on a global supply chain for its materials. And rather than stockpiling it relies on just-in-time deliveries to meet its needs, a practice that could prove disastrous during a major conflict.

The study's chief conclusion was that "the design, structure, and operation of the National Defense Stockpile render it ineffective in responding to modern needs and threats." It cited three major threats to the supply of materials critical to the national defense:

- Increased demand from around the world for mineral commodities and materials.
- Diminished domestic supply and processing capability along with greater dependence on foreign sources.
- Higher risk of and uncertainty about supply disruptions owing to the fragmentation of global supply chains.

The NRC's recommendation called for the establishment of a new system for managing the supply of strategic materials. Maintaining a materials inventory would be just one of the many tools available to a defense-materials management system. The new system would use all available tools to support and stabilize robust supply chains in the increasingly changeable and global environment for materials supply, including the option of partnering with private industry as well as for outsourcing and offshoring.

The report was published at a time when prices for many strategic materials had been rising sharply due to soaring demand from China. Rhenium, prized for its heat-resistant qualities, which allow jet engines to operate at high speeds, rose 1,000 percent, for instance. With hindsight, Congress' decision to pare down the national stockpile of strategic minerals has proved to be a false bargain.

No doubt influenced by the NRC's study, our military has suspended or limited sales of thirteen minerals, including beryllium, chromium, cobalt, ferrochrome, ferromanganese, germanium, iridium, niobium, platinum, tantalum, and tin. Since then, the Defense Department has expanded the list of resources it considers for stockpiling to sixty-eight, including specialty steels, lithium, and some rare earth elements. And more additions are expected, though the amount we will spend restocking the reserve will cost American taxpayers far more than they received as part of the Peace Dividend.

Moreover, under the archaic rules governing the strategic reserve, the military can't add to the stockpile list without first seeking congressional approval, a painfully slow process that can take as long as two years. This outdated practice leaves the United States vulnerable to potential shortages of supplies absolutely critical to national security as competition from China and other countries could severely reduce already limited availability.

Inadequate supplies of any one of a wide range of strategic minerals could prove to be our Achilles' heel in the event of war. If we find ourselves in a major confrontation with China or some other nation, our superiority in weapons systems, which have made America the world's undisputed superpower on land, at sea, and in the air, could be compromised if our forces are unable to field essential equipment in sufficient numbers due to a lack of key components that require strategic minerals to function.

Chapter 7

The Rise of Resource Nationalism

The scramble to secure fuel supplies and the minerals needed for a modern civilization will reshape nations' foreign policies, dissolve long-standing alliances, and lead to the creation of new ones. It will also make the world a much more dangerous place. Much like Europe a few short years before the outbreak of World War I, our seemingly peaceful, globalized economy is likely to give way to increasing economic competition and ultimately to a much more hostile world. Perhaps the best way to characterize this transition, which is already under way, as is the rise of resource nationalism, or at least a new age of mercantilism.

In a nutshell, resource nationalism entails state control of a commodity to achieve political goals. In years past, before the age of scarcity, resource nationalism typically would take the form of a government monopolizing an industry or at least holding a dominant stake, such as Saudi Aramco with oil or Chile's Codelco with copper, with the idea of maximizing the return on a nation's natural wealth. Such resource nationalism obviously still exists, such as Bolivia with lithium or Russia with oil and natural gas. Another less commonly practiced form of resource nationalism was the European state energy companies of the 1960s and 1970s that went out across the world in search of resources. (After years of mismanagement they were later privatized.)

The new resource nationalism is a whole other animal. Rather than seeking to generate the highest return on an asset, it endeavors to maximize a nation's access to a commodity. China's actions to secure materials in Africa are a prime example.

By leveraging low-interest government-guaranteed loans and subsidized support for Chinese construction firms building infrastructure in Africa, something no other country is doing, the Chinese government can maintain substantial control over the entire continent, effectively shutting out the United States and other nations. China is repeating this pattern in Afghanistan with the development of the Aynak copper field (which we discussed in chapter 4), and elsewhere in the world. It has had less success with this approach in Latin America, where infrastructure is already in place and more often than not the sellers want cash for their resources.

In order to secure the resources they will need in coming years, nations around the world are more commonly likely to hoard their own natural resources so they can continue to produce more valuable exports.

As we discussed earlier, China may soon cease all exports of rare earth elements—minerals that are critical to a wide range of technologies, including defense. This is a prime example of resource nationalism in action. Instead of letting the free market dictate what and how much of an item consumers can buy, China is reserving resources for its exclusive use or, for now at least, requiring that foreign manufacturers set up shop in China to gain access to the prized minerals (aiding the transfer of important technologies to the Middle Kingdom).

And as we saw in September 2010, the communist government is also prepared to use access to resources as a foreign policy tool.

China has been increasingly bellicose with its neighbors in recent years, and with the United States for that matter, about territorial waters in the South China and East China seas, where claimed exclusive national economic zones overlap. In addition to fish, these waters contain sizable deposits of oil and natural gas, as well as minerals that may one day be mined. Unfortunately, China is in no way inclined to share those resources with its neighbors.

This became all too clear after a Chinese fishing trawler rammed not one but two Japanese coast guard ships in the space of forty minutes in disputed waters near what it calls the Diaoyu Islands in the East China Sea. Known as the Senkaku Islands in the Land of the Rising Sun, which has administered the tiny, uninhabited specks of land since 1895, they're also claimed by the People's Republic (as part of the wayward province of Taiwan) and are considered a "core national interest" whose ownership dates to "ancient times," though outside of China that claim is considered a bit flimsy.

Clearly the Chinese were looking to pick a fight, and they used the fishing trawler as its pretext. The Japanese initially detained the boat's crew, though later released everyone but the ship's captain. Incensed, China demanded the captain's immediate release as well, and threatened that the failure to do so would result in severe consequences for Japan. When Japan failed to comply, China flexed its muscles by blocking exports of rare earth elements to Japan.

Rather than ordering an official halt to the exports, which would have given its rival solid grounds to file a complaint with the World Trade Organization, China simply "asked" its REE companies to temporarily delay shipments to Japan in patriotic support of the incarcerated fishing trawler captain while the government worked to resolve the spat. One REE producer, China Rare Earth Holdings, later admitted that more was at work in creating the de facto ban to Japan in that a local branch of the Chinese trade ministry stopped issuing export licenses during this time. The Chinese government went a step further, conducting spot inspections of goods bound for Japan as well as all goods arriving at ports from Japan, slowing trade considerably in the process.

Japan was already smarting from China's sharp reduction in REE exports several months before, so the move did the trick. Lacking another source for the rare earths needed for a wide range of products, and with its economy growing only just enough not to be classified as in recession, Japan acquiesced and put the captain on a plane, though in a face-saving gesture it refused to meet China's demands to foot the repair bill on the fishing trawler.

While Japan blinked this time around, it may not in the future, given the oil and natural gas reserves that are at stake in the East China Sea. China, meanwhile, will continue to strengthen its deepwater navy, which will put it in better position to exert its will in the region. The dispute between the two countries is not something Americans should readily dismiss. That's because under the Treaty of Mutual Cooperation and Security between Japan and the United States, we could be drawn into the fight should it come to open conflict in the future.

If such a scenario seems far-fetched, we would remind you again of the consensus view prior to the outbreak of World War I. Harvard historian Niall Ferguson, who has written extensively on the subject, had this to say in the March/April 2005 issue of *Foreign Affairs*:

It may seem excessively pessimistic to worry that this scenario could somehow repeat itself—that our age of globalization could collapse just as our grandparents' did. But it is worth bearing in mind that, despite numerous warnings issued in the early twentieth century about the catastrophic consequences of a war among the European great powers, many people—not least investors, a generally well-informed class—were taken completely by surprise by the outbreak of World War I. The possibility is as real today as it was in 1915 that globalization, like the *Lusitania*, could be sunk.

The last age of globalization resembled the current one in numerous ways. It was characterized by relatively free trade, limited restrictions on migration, and hardly any regulation of capital flows. Inflation was low. A wave of technological innovation was revolutionizing the communications and energy sectors; the world first discovered the joys of the telephone, the radio, the internal combustion engine, and paved roads. The U.S. economy was the biggest in the world, and the development of its massive internal market had become the principal source of business innovation. China was opening up, raising all kinds of expectations in the West, and Russia was growing rapidly.

Pressured by the need for energy and other resources, and with the United States stretched militarily and strapped financially, China (and other countries for that matter) is likely to be more prone to risk-taking moves to gain desired concessions. Certainly a sudden disruption in the dwindling supply of oil and gas, say as a result of a coup in the Kingdom of Saudi Arabia, might embolden the Chinese to forcefully seize assets. But even a seemingly minor incident could rapidly blossom into a devastating conflict.

For now, though, China can throw its weight around without having to resort to open conflict. Perhaps as a result of its success with Japan, shortly thereafter Beijing temporarily extended its unofficial export ban on rare earths to include the United States and the EU. This was in response to a complaint the United States brought to the World Trade Organization against China's subsidizing its clean tech industry (a policy we argue Washington should employ as well), to the detriment of competing companies in the West that don't receive government support. By the end of October, China had resumed shipments of rare earths abroad, lifting its undeclared embargo, all the while contending that it would never use rare earths as a bargaining chip.

Keep in mind that China's exploiting its monopoly position in rare earths to gain concessions from other countries is likely only just the beginning. In time we expect that the People's Republic will exercise similar tactics using the other metals discussed in these pages as bargaining chips. And that time may come quite soon. For instance, China is the world's largest exporter of silver and its third largest producer (after Peru and Mexico). Silver is essential for solar energy production, among other things, and as we showed in chapter 4, it too is increasingly in short supply. So the country's roughly 40 percent drop in silver exports in 2010 should be viewed with serious apprehension. At the very least, further reductions in China's silver exports will drive prices much higher. And due to the important role silver plays in myriad industrial applications as well as alternative energy, it is a prime candidate for China to use as a trump card to see that its demands are met. And silver is just one of many examples we can cite.

Projecting Its Power

As we document throughout this book, the overriding objective of China's foreign policy is to secure the resources it needs to fuel its economy. Part and parcel with this policy, Beijing is developing its military capabilities to ensure that the country's supply chain will not be disrupted. And it has made great strides in this effort. China's rapid growth in recent decades has afforded the ample funding for the modernization of its military, which today is both well trained and equipped with state-of-the-art weapons systems. As a result the military balance in East Asia has tilted significantly in recent years and will continue to shift in China's favor.

According to the U.S. Department of Defense's 2010 *Quadrennial Defense Review Report*, which assesses the threats and challenges our nation faces, "China is developing and fielding large numbers of advanced medium-range ballistic and cruise missiles, new attack submarines equipped with advanced weapons, increasingly capable long-range air defense systems, electronic warfare and computer network attack capabilities, advanced fighter aircraft, and counter-space systems."

The country's navy has the largest force of principal combatants, submarines, and amphibious warfare ships in Asia, with some seventy-five principal combatant ships, more than sixty submarines, fifty-five medium and large amphibious ships, and roughly eighty-five missile-equipped patrol craft. It is expected that China will continue to expand its military considerably in the coming years, with the objective of developing the capability to operate in "distant waters" to protect its interests. To this end, it is likely to begin to deploy multiple aircraft carriers in the coming decade, along with accompanying support ships. It has already begun to train pilots to operate fixed-wing aircraft from carriers. And it has begun flight tests of an advanced stealth fighter that reportedly includes breakthrough features to rival America's F-22 Raptor.

Just how much China is committing in annual expenditures for the expansion of its military is open to debate due to the communist government's lack of accounting transparency. Drawing from Sun Tzu's sixth-century-BC playbook, the country puts a strong emphasis on deception at all levels: tactical, operational, strategic, and budgetary.

China's military development is ostensibly subordinate to and in the service of the country's overall economic development. But there's reason to believe it is preparing for the day when it will be willing and able to exert force to meet its economic needs. While Beijing announces an

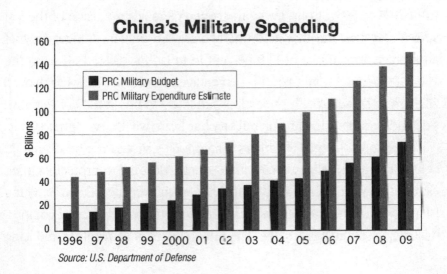

China's Military Spending

Legend:
- PRC Military Budget
- PRC Military Expenditure Estimate

Y-axis: $ Billions (0, 20, 40, 60, 80, 100, 120, 140, 160)

X-axis: 1996 97 98 99 2000 01 02 03 04 05 06 07 08 09

Source: U.S. Department of Defense

annual military budget that's officially around 2 percent of the country's gross domestic product, it is widely acknowledged among Sino observers, including the U.S. Department of Defense, that the country's defense spending is far higher—as much as triple the official figure. That suggests the country is spending a greater percentage of its GDP on defense than the United States. But even this doesn't tell the whole story.

Remember that China is still a command economy. The communist government can shift resources from civilian use to the military at the drop of a hat as it sees fit, with no scrutiny from the media or vocal complaints from its citizens. Also, the numbers being thrown around for China's military outlays are in nominal terms. If you adjust the country's spending relative to its comparative purchasing power, its military expenditures jump by 80 percent or more. And its military expenditures are increasing at a rate that is at least commensurate with the pace of its economic growth.

A *Kyodo News* story in July 2010 cited an internal report from the People's Liberation Army that indicated China's military expenditures were expected to double to 1.41 trillion yuan by 2020 and triple to 2.30 trillion yuan by 2030. That forecast was based on the assumption that its gross domestic product will grow by 6 percent annually to 2020 and 5 percent from 2021 to 2030. Considering the country's rapid expansion of the last several decades and that its officially disclosed military budget grew at an average annual rate of 11.8 percent in inflation-adjusted terms in the 2000–09 period, more than two percentage points more per year than its GDP grew, those growth projections are likely to be on the conservative side and Beijing's spending on military hardware will be even greater.

The growing might of China's armed forces should not be dismissed lightly. There's nothing wrong with a country desiring to protect its interests, but as we've seen in its dispute with Japan over the Diaoyu/Senkaku Islands, China may not always be willing to settle for a peaceful compromise when so much is at stake. The United States, meanwhile, is reducing its military expenditures in an effort to get its financial house in order—at a time when our need for a strong military is as great as ever.

Fighting for Pole Position

The practice of resource nationalism and territorial claims is by no means limited to China. It's a race we expect will accelerate going forward, and it's likely to be quite overt, in the manner of the European empire-building of the fifteenth to nineteenth centuries.

The lure of vast mineral wealth in the Arctic prompted Russia in 2007 to plant a rustproof titanium flag on the sea floor at the North Pole, an area of the globe that is generally not considered a part of any country's territory and is administered by the United Nations International Seabed Authority. Current international law grants countries an exclusive economic zone of two hundred nautical miles beyond their land borders. If a country can prove that the structure of the continental shelf is similar to the geologic structure within its territory, that zone can be extended.

In 2001 Moscow took its case to the UN, claiming that the waters off its northern coast were an extension of its maritime territory on the grounds that the subsurface Lomonosov Ridge (which extends across the North Pole toward Greenland) was an extension of its continental territory. That claim was rejected by the UN, but it prompted several other countries with territories bordering the Arctic—including the United States, Canada, Denmark, and Norway—to launch competing claims to the region. Canada's foreign minister, Lawrence Cannon, indicated the seriousness of his government's claim to the area by stating that establishing sovereignty in the Arctic was the country's "top foreign policy priority."

Russia also maintains a permanent floating research station in the Chukchi Sea, north of the Bering Strait, between Russia and the United States, to bolster its claim to an area believed to be rich in oil and natural gas deposits. According to the U.S. Geological Survey, the Arctic contains an estimated ninety billion barrels of undiscovered, technically recoverable, oil; 1,670 trillion cubic feet of technically recoverable natural gas; and forty-four billion barrels of technically recoverable natural gas liquids. That's roughly 30 percent of the world's estimated undiscovered oil and gas, a prize many might see as worth fighting for, which may be what prompted Russia to announce a $678 billion military spending package in early 2011. A quarter of that money will be allocated to the country's Pacific fleet, with plans to add twenty new ships, including helicopter carriers, several frigates, attack submarines, and missile subs. The beefed-up fleet will allow Russia to better defend its Arctic interests against any and all comers.

At the opposite end of the earth, Antarctica too is thought to contain tremendous riches. The continental shelf under the Weddell and Ross seas, for instance, is estimated to contain 50 billion barrels of oil, while the Transantarctic Mountains have known deposits of coal, iron ore, gold, silver, copper, zinc, nickel, lead, tin, platinum, and other important minerals.

Antarctica, however, is off-limits for the exploitation of natural resources under the 1991 Protocol on Environmental Protection to the Antarctic Treaty, which explicitly forbids "any activity relating to mineral resources, other than scientific research." The ban won't expire until 2048. Nevertheless, twenty-nine countries have established research bases there. China, for one, has expanded its Antarctic operations in recent years, setting up multiple research facilities. Included in its official research priorities there is investigating the potential of Antarctica's untapped resources.

How the continent's spoils will be divided when resources are far more scarce than they are today is anyone's guess at this point. The original 1959 Antarctic Treaty froze the territorial claims of seven nations (Argentina, Australia, Chile, France, New Zealand, Norway, and the United Kingdom) and banned military activity there. At the time the treaty was signed, the United States and the Soviet Union hedged their bets by each filing reservations against the restriction on new claims on the continent.

When push comes to shove, those territorial claims are likely to be revived. And it's hard to see how the matter will be resolved peacefully with so much at stake.

A Taxing Issue

China has invoked the need to "conserve the environment and exhaustible natural resources" to enact measures that are blatant steps toward resource nationalism. While its curbs on rare earth minerals exports have garnered the media's attention, Chinese restrictions on exports of raw materials go much further. Complaints have been brought by the United States, Europe, and Mexico to the World Trade Organization for the country's curbs on raw materials including, but not limited to, coke, zinc, and magnesium, for all three of which it's the world's largest producer. The Chinese government levies a 40 percent duty on coke, for instance, and imposes export quotas on the mineral. Coke is used in the production of steel, and the measures are harmful to foreign steel manufacturers while aiding domestic Chinese producers. The WTO has set up a special panel to investigate the claims, but so far no action has been taken against the country.

Taxes on resources are a popular tool in other countries as well. In early 2010, Kevin Rudd, the Australian prime minister, floated a plan to impose a 40 percent supertax on mining company profits as a means of maximizing the country's wealth. The idea proved unpopular and Rudd was soon drummed out of office by his own party. His replacement, Julia Gillard, proposed a drastically scaled-down version of the tax that was limited to iron ore, coal, oil, and natural gas (which represent three-quarters of Australia's exports), but it's likely not the last we'll hear of such a tax from Australia.

Kazakhstan, the largest oil producer in Central Asia and a major exporter of chrome, copper, and iron ore, recently reintroduced an export duty on oil, with plans to follow that with a tax on exports of metals. Though the export duty on oil is relatively modest at a fixed $40 per metric ton (about $5.50 per barrel), it will open the door to higher tariffs down the road.

The list of countries with such export duties goes on. The lure of tax revenue rolling in (that doesn't come out of constituents' pockets) can be a powerful incentive for politicians to act, which gives us reason to believe that higher resource taxes are assured on virtually all minerals.

At some point, higher taxes will give way to countries hoarding their natural wealth. That day may be closer than most people realize.

Since independence from Great Britain in 1947, India has imposed protectionist measures to insulate its populace from outside competition, most notably in the textile industry. While many of those protectionist measures have fallen by the wayside in the last several decades, India is still mindful of shielding itself from neocolonial threats.

In a country notably short on many resources (other than human capital), India's government is intent on holding on to one commodity it does have in abundance: iron ore. India is the world's third-largest iron ore exporter. But government officials are worried it won't have enough ore to meet its own steel mills' needs in a few short years and is now considering banning exports altogether.

India produced about 230 million metric tons of iron ore in fiscal 2009–10 and exported nearly half of that to China. To discourage exports and capitalize on the doubling in prices in the previous year of what it does sell abroad, in 2010 the Indian government hiked its iron ore export duty to 15 percent from 10 percent. Raising the export duty serves as a convenient way for the government to fill its coffers. But the impetus for the duty increase (and possible export ban) has to do with national interests.

The Indian steel ministry has set a production target of 124 million metric tons per year by 2012–13, more than double the current annual production of around 54 million metric tons. Achieving that target will require a heck of a lot more iron ore. In anticipation, in July 2010 the southern Indian state of Karnataka, an important ore-producing region, went a step further by banning iron ore exports. As a result, India's iron ore shipments are expected to decline by 35 to 40 percent in fiscal year 2010–11. The impact of this won't be felt just in China but the world over as the reduced supply will drive up not only the cost of iron ore, but of finished steel as well.

In recent years the high cost of fossil fuels has priced many countries out of the market. With inadequate supplies on hand, load shedding, a sobriquet for frequent power outages, has become commonplace in many parts of the world. Even some of the more affluent countries have not been immune. One such country is South Africa, which at the time of this writing is considering banning the export of even low-grade coal so that it will have enough to power its own utility plants, if only for part of a given day.

For the time being, Russia will continue to derive a substantial portion of its GDP from the export of energy and other raw materials, with China a top customer. But at some point the leaders in Moscow will likewise wake up and realize that Russia too needs to reserve those commodities for its own development.

Despite its vast mineral wealth and its fairly well-educated population, Russia's infrastructure development is sadly lacking. For instance, the country's population is three and a half times larger than Spain's and its land area is thirty-three times larger, yet it has only about the same number of miles of paved roads. That's not to mention the qualitative differences in the two countries' road systems. Driving the 420 miles between Russia's two most important cities, Moscow and St. Petersburg, a distance shorter than the trip from Boston to Washington, D.C., is ill-advised even in the best of conditions because the roads are narrow and poorly maintained. Just driving from the center of Moscow to the city's airport can routinely take six hours. This lack of infrastructure is in large part why the hundreds of wildfires that raged across western Russia in the summer of 2010 were so devastating. Officials estimated that smog from the fires, coupled with a record heat wave, were responsible for the deaths of thousands as whole villages were burned to the ground in the wildfires.

Any attempt by the government to bring Russia's infrastructure from its current state to a level on par with Western Europe while also developing alternative energy will require every last pound of materials Russia has in its soil. Eventually, Russian national interests will trump a desire for export revenue.

Until those resources are no longer available, however, China will continue to buy everything it can lay its hands on, from Russia and every other country willing to sell, even at much higher prices. With the yuan likely to appreciate meaningfully in the next several years, this will increase China's purchasing power, softening the blow. But the United States will have to contend with not only higher resource prices, but an emasculated currency that will make our pain all the more severe.

Resource Liberalism

Some would maintain that this new resource nationalism is already being practiced by market-driven democracies as well. How else do you explain the decision of CNOOC (the state-owned China National Offshore Oil Corporation) to walk away from a bid to acquire Unocal in 2005 after intense political pressure from the U.S. government? In the same vein, in 2009 the Australian government blocked an attempt by China Nonferrous Metal Company to acquire a majority interest in Lynas Corporation, an Aussie rare earth elements miner. That same year, the Canberra government also nixed China's Wuhan Iron and Steel Company's proposed joint venture with miner Western Plains. Opposition to each of these deals was based on national security grounds, but was something more at play here?

Jeffrey D. Wilson, professor of international relations at the Australian National University, has persuasively argued that his country's actions to prevent Chinese acquisition of mining companies there was actually based on economic liberalism rather than nationalism. Chinese acquisitions are being blocked because they are seen as being potentially anticompetitive. This same argument can be extended to the United States and other market-driven economies that have stood in the way of China's resource-buying spree. Wilson points out several characteristics of Chinese foreign direct investment in iron ore mining projects that differentiate the nature of those investments from those made by publicly traded Western companies:

Recent Chinese FDI [foreign direct investment] into the Australian mining industry is qualitatively unlike investment from other sources in a variety of ways. First, it is driven primarily by demand from the Chinese steel industry for raw materials, and thus is concentrated in just two mining sectors—iron ore and coking coal. Second, these investments have largely been made by SOEs [state-owned enterprises] rather than private firms, typically either mining groups or steel mills themselves, and usually with some kind of governmental financial assistance. Third, they arguably originate from a state-backed agenda that aims to use FDI to influence transactions in international iron ore and coking coal markets.

Rather than an attempt to subject market-based economic processes to political control for national developmental purposes, Wilson sees Australia's bids to block Chinese takeovers as "a defensive move against the potential for non-market behavior resulting from the state-directed character of the Chinese investors, rather than any national program to politically control minerals trade and investment. . . . It is more than just a negation of resource nationalist policies; and instead involves a state relying primarily on international market mechanisms for the development of its natural resources, through relatively unrestricted trade and investment policies."

In time, as the growing scarcity of resources is recognized for what it is, we expect this liberalism on the part of the United States, Australia, and other nations to give way to the resource nationalism China is fully engaged in already. If we don't, we may regret it.

Chapter 8

Why Dealing with Declining Resources Is Easier for China

Critics of our work will claim that America does not really have to worry about losing an energy race to China because of our vast superiority in technology. It is part of the American ethos that we are head and shoulders above other countries when it comes to technology, and that this lead will provide the path to future energy and national security. But before accepting this view let's take a little closer look at Chinese technology.

Certainly we won't claim China has an edge in technology. Indeed, the Chinese have basically been copycats—though exceedingly good ones. Of course, China has produced some utterly brilliant scientists, including Qian Xuesen. Born in China, Qian, who died in 2009 at the age of ninety-eight, spent the formative part of his academic life at MIT and Cal Tech. During the 1930s and 1940s, he along with several colleagues at Cal

Tech provided the scientific basis that would underlie America's space program. During the communist scare of the 1950s, however, Qian lost his security clearance, and in 1955 he returned to China. When he died, *Nature* quoted him as saying that in China he missed the creative spark that characterized U.S. science. Still, the Chinese were superb students, and Qian became known as the father of the Chinese space program.

The Chinese philosophy can be summed up as: Search for better, but meanwhile go all-out with what you have. Julian Wong, a Fulbright scholar who studied technology and energy issues in Beijing and is widely considered to be one of the world's leading experts on the relationship between Chinese technology and China's energy policy, described it as follows in his written testimony before the U.S.-China Economic and Security Review Commission on July 14, 2010:

> To achieve its goals of indigenous innovation, China's government has adopted a model of "import-absorb-digest-re-innovate." Thus, the early stages of all technology development include heavy reliance on foreign technologies. These technology transfer opportunities sometimes result from intergovernmental cooperation—as was the case with energy conservation technologies made available to China through the auspices of the Japanese Green Aid Plan between 1992 and 2003. They can also result from purely commercial negotiations, as in the case of Goldwind, a Chinese wind company that acquired much of its intellectual property and know-how by licensing foreign technologies and ultimately outright acquiring a German wind company. Goldwind was virtually unheard of in 2008. Now it has gone public and is the world's eighth-largest wind turbine manufacturer.
>
> Today, China continues to increase its R&D capacity by welcoming expertise from Western multinational high-tech corporations. Applied Materials, the world's biggest supplier of solar manufacturing equipment, has opened a new major R&D facility

in China and has relocated its chief technology officer from Silicon Valley to China. Applied Materials' move follows on the heels of DuPont, another American company that expanded its solar R&D facilities in Shanghai last summer, and IBM, which opened its R&D facility for software control systems for high-speed rail in Beijing around the same time.

Consistently, my colleagues and I heard from several foreign business executives during our April visit that these companies are choosing to locate R&D centers in China because that is where both the manufacturing infrastructure and the ultimate demand for these products is, and that it makes economic and business sense to conduct R&D close to other parts of the value chain. But this trend also represents a potential threat to American innovation because clean-energy manufacturing activities and markets are growing more rapidly abroad.

As the statement implies, the Chinese have very little pride in ownership when it comes to originating a critical technology. Rather, they have a goal, and they are determined to achieve it the fastest way possible. If technology breakthroughs in the United States can bring them closer to energy independence, so be it.

Days later, *Nature*'s July 18, 2010, issue included an article entitled "A New Strategy for Energy Innovation." Its major point was to urge the following: "Washington should make use of a powerful policy tool that it has largely neglected: public sector procurement. Procurements by the US Department of Defense (DOD) were the foundation for major waves of innovation after the Second World War." As an example, the authors noted that "government purchases of integrated-circuit chips in the 1960s fostered advances in microelectronics at least as much as did government-funded R&D."

Major purchases by government help push technological advances in part because they force companies to concentrate on economies of scale.

On this front the Chinese are way ahead of us. By establishing themselves as the largest manufacturers of many alternative energy technologies, they continue to get the biggest orders. And with every large order comes the chance to improve their cost advantage—the chance to learn new methods of further reducing costs. It is a virtuous circle that, unless checked, suggests the Chinese will become ever more technologically dominant in alternative energies.

Along these lines we were struck by a Bloomberg story that appeared on July 23, 2010, with the headline "Rutgers' Chinese Solar Panels Show Clean-Energy Shift." The story points out that the New Jersey–based university had chosen a Chinese firm to supply its campus with solar panels, because the Chinese produce panels more cheaply than anyone else. The reporter, Stuart Biggs, noted, "China is slashing prices and moving to dominate solar energy in the way Japanese manufacturers ruled consumer electronics decades ago." The Chinese, in other words, are finding ways of reducing costs further by being the low-cost provider. This makes them dual winners: They win in the profit column, but far more important over the longer term, they win when it comes to energy security as well. And, of course, there is all the difference in the world between consumer electronics and renewable energies. We can run our civilization without a great deal of consumer electronics, but without renewable energies most everything is kaput.

The Chinese are not enamored of quantum leaps forward in science or technology. Instead, they focus on applying methods that work— sometimes in novel ways, sometimes in more practical ways than are currently being used. In its July 23, 2010, posting, the excellent blog *China Dialog* carried two articles by several British professors who gave examples of what the Chinese are doing to conserve energy, protect the environment, and generate new sources of energy. They listed seven such innovations. Each is a relatively minor reapplication of knowledge that is readily available. For example, a Chinese nongovernmental organization has established methods allowing it to become socially acceptable for poor farmers to use biogas. Others include the development of electric bikes and the use of less energy-intensive, relatively low-tech approaches to air-conditioning. Government support for these "technologies" virtually guarantees massive savings of energy and large reductions of carbon—all achieved without any major technology breakthrough.

The Chinese are ruthlessly practical. In evaluating technologies, they'll look at the long-term worth to their economy. This means that in a wake of a disastrous offshore oil spill, they would likely continue to explore for crude as long as they concluded that the resulting long-term gains in energy security would be greater than any ecological damage. Indeed, not long after the Macondo disaster, the Chinese cleaned up after an oil spill caused by a pipeline explosion that likely did even more ecological harm than the massive spill in the Gulf of Mexico. There is no talk of a moratorium on anything concerned with pipelines—despite the disaster, it is all systems go.

This has been the case with rare earth minerals, which are horribly toxic to mine but whose long-term worth, under the cold calculations made by the Chinese, well exceed the near-term costs. And, of course, the same applies to recycling metals from electronic parts, another highly toxic process whose long-term payoff is very high. It is no surprise that within a decade or less, the Chinese will surpass America in nuclear power.

An American Myth

One of the great American myths is that technology will always save the day. One of the most prescient articles that touched on this topic appeared in the September/October 1995 issue of *Foreign Affairs*. The article was penned by a brilliant Japanese minister, Eisuke Sakakibara, who in 2010 retired from many years of distinguished service in the Japanese government. Sakakibara argued that the end of the cold war was not so much the triumph of one civilization over another but rather a victory in how materialism or progressivism can best prosper. The cold war, then, was really a civil war between the United States and the Soviet Union that said nothing about whether progressivism itself is the ultimate civilization. His comments on China nearly a generation later are telling:

> However, a more fundamental issue is whether or not democracy and neoclassical capitalism are the only or ultimate goals, or even whether any goal needs to be established. China has set its sights on establishing a socialist market economy and, relative to Russia, has so far succeeded in introducing many facets of market mechanisms without major economic or political upheaval. While it may still be too early to pass final judgment on the recent Chinese experiment, it does at least provide a realistic alternative goal and methodology.

Later on in the same article Sakakibara describes what he regards as the limits of Western technology:

> The knowledge that humans have accumulated about nature and human beings themselves is quite limited. Because natural science tries to understand vast systems from only minute observations, it will never be able to assess accurately the impact of human activity on the environment, much less solve environmental problems through technological innovation. Technological progress may, in a small way, compensate for some human impact on nature or, at best, delay the destruction for a very short time. The progressivists' confidence in human competence and technology could properly be termed a myth because there is no logical reason to believe such path-breaking technological change will occur. It is akin to believing that someday the savior will come down to earth in the form of technological innovation and for some reason reverse all the problems that past progress has wrought. This myth of technological innovation parallels unswerving faith in economic growth.

If this quote evokes the work of social psychologist Richard Nisbett, co-director of the Culture and Cognition program at the University of Michigan, it is not accidental. The Western way is a detailed focus and analysis of central aims at the expense of the context. Sakakibara's point is that this is not a method suited to the complexities of the natural world. We give examples below, but for now simply contrast America's obsession with trying to innovate with a focus on individual parts with the Chinese focus on "import-absorb-digest-re-innovate." Whatever the West discovers the Chinese redefine in a societal context. This applies to everything from solar energy to monetary policy (see chapter 10). Innovation for the sake of innovation does not serve a goal. It is always a question of going with what they have—or perhaps better said, whatever they can get their hands on—and doing it in a way that maximizes societal good.

It follows from Nisbett's experiments and Sakakibara's observations that the West's unyielding focus on detail would go hand in hand with a focus on machines that are expert at manipulating details. And so it is not surprising that the past half century has marked in the West the apotheosis of the computer. It is this blind faith in the power of technology and technology's major tool, the computer, which keeps us in search of the magic bullet—a transformative technology that in a coruscating second will solve all our resource and security problems. Such faith isn't innocuous. Rather, it poses a massive threat to our future. For as long as we believe in the "magic" of technology and computers, America will remain tragically unable to solve the problems of resource shortages that could cripple us within the next decade. In the meantime China will continue to make the best of whatever is out there—and as they have done so far in the area of alternative energies, they will leave us in the dust.

The True Believers

For years we've been reading about all the wondrous gains that computers have made, to the point where many believe it's only a matter of time before computers trump humans in matters intellectual. Some, in fact, believe we're already there.

The inventor and futurist Ray Kurzweil is one of the better-known advocates of the ultimate superiority of machines over human intellect. In his book *The Singularity Is Near* he argues that human and machine intelligence will merge—perhaps within the next fifty years—with breathtaking changes, a quantum leap in evolution.

What makes Kurzweil and many others credible are the seemingly growing accomplishments of artificial intelligence. One presumed milestone was the 1997 chess match between then world chess champion Garry Kasparov and the IBM computer Deep Blue, which was declared the winner. We commented on this match in our book *Defying the Market* (1999), explaining why, contrary to common belief, the outcome in no way demonstrated that Deep Blue had outthought Kasparov—rather, the computer simply had the advantage of not getting physically tired or getting psyched out by an opponent.

More recently, in the summer of 2010 the *New York Times Magazine* ran a cover story noting that once again IBM had built a computer that could outthink humans. In this case, the computer was dubbed "Watson" and had been programmed to play the game of *Jeopardy!* (If you've never seen it, *Jeopardy!* is a long-running quiz show that tests contestants' knowledge of trivia. The twist is that instead of being asked a question, they are given the answer and must supply the question. For instance, a contestant might have to supply the correct question for: "He hit sixty home runs in 1927." The correct response, of course: "Who was Babe Ruth?")

Initially, Watson, which could make around half a trillion calculations a second, right up there with the fastest computers, was a poor competitor. But after several years, with three dedicated programmers, the machine proved to be superior to *Jeopardy!* reigning champions.

When a mathematician friend drew our attention to this article, trumpeting this new triumph of artificial intelligence—a computer that could beat trivia experts!—our response was to wonder what Watson might say if asked how to repair a massive leak in the ocean floor that was threatening the entire Gulf coast. Of course, no computer in the world, it turned out, had an answer to that one. Instead, it was good old-fashioned human ingenuity—using computers as important tools but not as guiding lights—that ultimately supplied a solution.

This raises a very basic point: Have we been putting our research monies to the best possible use? So much time and money have been devoted to making computers and the Internet operate at ever faster speeds. But what have we really gained from this? What if, for instance, computers were only half as fast—and we'd used the money instead to carry out basic research into oceanography? We think such a trade-off would have made the world far better off.

The fastest computers today can perform several quadrillion calculations per second, an almost incomprehensibly fast speed. The problem is that even a speed of a quintillion calculations per second—a thousand times faster than today's top speed—still would be dwarfed by the complexity of the problems nature is serving up to us today. Moreover, natural products such as metals—never mind complex organisms—can't be duplicated by an equation or algorithm generated by any current or conceivable computer.

An example that we offered in our 1999 book, relating to the discovery of high-temperature superconductivity, is still telling. For many years it was thought that superconductivity (the passage of electricity through a metal without any resistance) could occur only at temperatures near absolute zero. Then in the mid-1980s a group of scientists discovered that superconductivity could occur at temperatures that, while exceedingly cold, were, in scientific terms, still well above absolute zero. Superconductivity near absolute zero requires liquid helium, while the new high-temperature materials needed to be cooled "only" to the level of liquid nitrogen. And while this still precluded nearly all applications, including the long-distance transmission of electricity, the 1986 Nobel Prize in Physics was awarded the scientists who had created the material capable of high-temperature superconductivity.

At the time of the Nobel award, the press was filled with forecasts of trains traveling 300 miles an hour or faster via superconducting; of storing electricity through superconductivity rings; and, best of all, of the resistance-free transmitting of electricity. It seemed that technology had taken a big step forward, including finding a solution to our future energy problems.

So far, however, the achievement has had a very disappointing aftermath. The catch was that the forecasts all assumed it was just a matter of time before improvements in technology would allow us to manufacture materials capable of superconductivity much past the temperature of liquid nitrogen. Indeed, some projected that superconductivity at room temperatures was just around the corner. The assumption was that a largely adventitious discovery of materials conducive to higher-temperature superconductivity would quickly lead to an understanding of the phenomenon and therefore to an ability to create materials capable of superconductivity at ever higher temperatures. But this assumption proved naïve indeed.

More than a generation later there have been a few more serendipitous discoveries—other materials have been found that are also capable of superconductivity at temperatures perhaps a couple of degrees higher than the original materials. But there has been no quantum leap: To achieve superconductivity, we still need liquid nitrogen and the energy to keep nitrogen liquid. For all but a handful of applications this is not an energy-efficient exercise, much less a civilization-changing revolution. Unfortunately, what we said more than a decade ago about superconductivity still stands today.

Of course, books can be written on the nature of superconductivity and on why raising the temperature at which it is possible has proved so elusive. But one enduring problem remains the factor we pinpointed in our earlier book: that science, rather than using the computer as a valuable but subordinate tool, has been misguidedly relying on it to create new science—something the computer is ill-equipped to do.

In the case of superconductivity this has meant that a disproportionate amount of research has gone into disciplines such as combinatorial chemistry. Computers generate endless combinations of chemicals based on the properties different chemicals possess. It might seem like a logical approach. The problem, though, is that no matter how many properties you can attribute to a particular material, it can't describe what happens when you combine that material with another one with different properties. Even seemingly subtle changes in any of the properties can significantly alter what the combined material can do.

Just as superconductivity was a serendipitous discovery (clearly it was not the result of chemical deduction but rather happenstance), so was another wondrous discovery, that of graphene. This carbon substance can be layered with widths measured in atoms, yet it is stronger than steel and a better conductor than copper. If graphene could be scaled into large sheets it would have the potential to be transformative—solve most of the world's resource problems. Unfortunately, the issues with graphene are the same as those with superconductivity. To scale this miraculous material will take a deep understanding of chemistry and physics, which is very unlikely to come from the shotgun approach to experimentation that is generated from high-throughput computer analysis.

It's relevant here to invoke a famous philosopher of science, Rudolf Carnap. One of his many brilliant insights, and one that today's scientists seem to overlook, is that there is theoretically no difference between a full understanding of a phenomenon and a prediction. This would mean, in other words, that if we truly understood the relationship between materials and superconductivity, we could accurately predict what materials will permit higher-temperature superconductivity.

Wanted: Ingenuity, Commitment, and Urgency

Computers, clearly, are adequate when it comes to relatively simple phenomena. For instance, computers have solved the game of checkers simply by virtue of their brute calculating ability. (As it turns out, if both sides are playing their best in checkers, the game will always end in a draw. Chess is a different story; see sidebar on page 134.) But when it comes to combining materials with virtually unlimited numbers of properties, the computer, no matter how fast, is outmanned—materials are simply too complex. And this takes us right back to our current dilemma: We live in a world with an ever more urgent need for a diminishing supply of metals and other materials that the computer can't duplicate.

Lu Ke, of the Chinese Academy of Sciences' Institute of Metal Research, writing in *Science* on April 16, 2010, noted that "metals are still the major workhorse of our society and will remain so in the future, thanks to unique properties that make them irreplaceable." Some of these properties, he says, include "toughness." Steels, for example, are the toughest known materials. Metals are uniform in all directions, and their properties are readily predictable. Barring a breakthrough in superconductivity, metals—in particular copper and aluminum—are the best long-range conductors of electricity. (Even if there were a breakthrough, the composite material would likely include copper and possibly silver.) Thankfully, metals also are recyclable, a consequence of their ability to maintain their integrity even at very high temperatures.

Lu also points out that metallic alloys or mixtures of metals and other materials are simple and predictable in their properties. Titanium alloys, for example, are both less dense and less tough than steel. But when it comes to properties that can't be derived from a straightforward combining of materials with known properties—as is the case with superconductivity— you can't expect to succeed simply through randomly combining different materials. And this explains why after nearly a quarter of a century of trying, we still haven't managed to produce materials that can be superconductive at temperatures much higher than was possible in 1986. To accomplish this would require a deep understanding of the underlying science, something we don't have. (Note that even with this deep understanding, we still might not be able to produce the requisite materials—that is, understanding is a necessary but not sufficient condition.)

Another top science publication, Britain's *Nature* runs a one-page sci-fi piece in each issue. The story in the June 17, 2010, issue posits a super-advanced civilization that is forced to reach out to a more primitive universe for help: Because of its advanced technologies, it was running out of silicon and phosphorus. Fiction, yes, but the point is well taken.

The flip side of the scientific failures we've talked about is scientific success. It's striking that the greatest scientific successes have resulted from human insight, not computers—such discoveries as the circulation of blood, the laws of heredity, and the elucidation of DNA, not to mention Darwin and Freud.

A 2005 book, *The Discoveries*, by Alan Lightman, reinforces the point. The book was billed as presenting the great breakthroughs in twentieth-century science. Lightman highlighted twenty-two such discoveries, ranging from Einstein's theory of special relativity to Heisenberg's uncertainty principle to Watson and Crick's discovery of the structure of DNA. The last chapter in the book—the twenty-second breakthrough—describes a discovery made in 1972. Thus, not one of these seminal scientific breakthroughs required or made use of exceptional computing power.

And incidentally, Lightman's book, perhaps inadvertently, makes another telling point. Many of the papers he presents have just one or two authors. Only two have more than three. In 2008, *Nature* did a study of its own papers and found that the number of authors for papers published in the 2000s was quadruple that for those published in 1950

Scientific papers have always contained two quantities—the increment of new science and the credit for its discovery. From the late 1600s until about 1920, the rule was one author per paper: an individual produced an increment of science and obtained a corresponding increment of credit. The symmetry was breached in the 1920s and diminished in the 1950s and largely abandoned by the 1980s. . . . The ruling convention of multiple authorship is that all authors shared in the work more or less equally and, if the

Major Discoveries of the 20th Century

Discovery	Number of Authors	Year
The Quantum	1	1900
Hormones	1	1902
Particle Nature of Light	1	1905
Special Relativity	1	1905
Nucleus of the Atom	1	1911
Size of the Cosmos	1	1912
Atomic Structure of Solid Matter	3	1912
Constitution of the Atom	1	1913
Communication Between Nerves	1	1921
Uncertainty Principle	1	1927
The Chemical Bond	1	1928
Expansion of the Universe	1	1929
Antibiotics	1	1929
Energy Production in Living Organisms	2	1937
Nuclear Fission	2	1939
Movability of Genes	2	1948
Structure of DNA	2	1953
Structure of Proteins	6	1960
Radio Waves from the Big Bang	2	1965
Unified Theory of Forces	1	1967
The Nature of Quarks	9	1969
Creation of Altered Forms of Life	3	1972

Source: The Discoveries *by Alan Lightman, authors of November 2010 issue of Nature*

first author or two takes the role of "first among equals," all listed authors take full credit for the contents of the paper. This is easy enough to swallow where three or four authors are concerned, harder when there are eight to 10 authors, and almost impossible with 20 or 50—let alone hundreds, as in some sequencing papers.

Why so many authors on today's scientific papers? There may be a lot of reasons, but certainly one necessary condition is the advent of the

Internet. In the old days—prior to 1980—mass and nearly instantaneous communication was not possible. As a result, papers were the creative and persistent work of one to several scientists. Can you imagine even a dozen scientists participating equally in developing a revolutionary idea about the creation of energy?

The sequencing of a gene, by contrast, isn't an insight, it is a description, and one that so far has not produced much in the way of new drugs or anything that has really bettered humanity. That is not surprising. We have determined that there are about 20,000 human genes, along with a mass of other genetic material. This other material, formerly known as "junk" DNA, is now recognized as playing an important, though ill-defined, role in creating organisms. But forget about junk DNA, just consider the 20,000 genes. These genes function not in isolation but in conjunction with one another. And their number of potential combinations far exceeds the number of elementary particles in the universe—and by an inconceivable margin exceeds the computing capacity of the largest imaginable computers. Likewise, what we say about humans applies with equal force to many other living organisms, even corn and wheat, which genetically speaking are incredibly complex. And even when it comes to organisms that really are simple enough to allow us to delineate all possible combinations of genes, we can't come anywhere close to explaining how those combinations interact with a nearly infinitely complex environment.

Steven Chu is a remarkably competent Energy Department head. He won a Nobel Prize in basic science (a computer-based analysis of how elementary particles behave) and is an exceptionally skilled administrator. In all ways he is a dedicated public servant. But he is also the product of today's views on science. Most of the research the department is sponsoring is for tweaking existing technologies—such as coming up with better combinations of materials for converting solar light into energy or better designs for nuclear plants.

These are all efforts that could no doubt make important changes at the margins. But the Energy Department is spending a relative pittance to support fundamental research. And it isn't making the kinds of distinctions vital to achieving a true game-changing breakthrough.

One of the department's divisions is dubbed ARPA (after the Defense Department's well-known DARPA), and it is designed to foster genuinely innovative ideas—the kind of revolutionary research essential to ensure our civilization's survival. As of this writing, funding has been temporarily completed, with a total of 117 projects being granted about $350 million in all, or about $3 million per project. If this doesn't sound like all that much, you could argue that with a lot less, Heisenberg managed to work out the equations that define quantum mechanics. It's not the amount of money that troubles us so much as the criteria that have been established for receiving the money.

Recipients of the funds include universities, small businesses, large businesses, national labs, and nonprofit institutions. That is, individuals or small groups working outside a major institution need not apply. Yet it is exactly these latter categories that have spawned much of the science that defines the modern world. And although we don't have any data, it's a good bet that it's individuals and small independent groups (who would lack access to the biggest computers) who are most likely to use the computer as a useful tool rather than as the be-all and end-all of their research efforts.

Computers, however powerful, aren't going to create new metals, and won't by themselves overcome the massive hurdles to creating a world powered by renewable energies. They only can help at the margins—increasing the amounts of materials that are recyclable, prolonging battery life, improving our ability to locate deposits of critical metals. But right now we seem to be betting the house on computer-based discoveries. How else can you explain our complacency toward the overwhelming problems we face? It has become axiomatic that science will continue to progress—perhaps at an exponential rate—and that solutions to our energy and resource problems are just around the corner. It's a false if comforting axiom that we have to abandon.

Our society's unwavering presumption that technology will solve our energy problems isn't the only obstacle we must overcome. Historian and anthropologist Joseph Tainter, whom we've cited earlier and in previous books, has pointed out that running into resource limits is often the major reason why advanced civilizations tend to fail. Their complexity becomes so overwhelming that the cost of any major program, whether it is the creation of new energy supplies or any other major project, becomes prohibitive. This is clearly seen with America today.

Consider the American Recovery and Reinvestment Act of 2009, the government's $787 billion stimulus package cobbled together to jump-start our economy when it was in the depths of the worst economic contraction since the Great Depression. Just $30 billion was allocated to the Department of Energy for energy research, a sad statement on America's commitment to achieving energy independence in and of itself. But because it takes so much time to fill out grant proposals and for those proposals to be evaluated, only a fifth of those funds had been spent a year and a half after the package was signed into law. Indeed, most of the money won't be spent for years—and it will be longer still, if ever, that we might actually make use of the results of any of the funded research.

Our government's inability to act swiftly in restocking the Department of Defense's strategic reserve of metals and minerals, which we discussed in chapter 6, is a good case in point. Health care and even education offer other examples of debilitating complexity in our society as well. In both areas, at most $20 billion intelligently spent could result in major advancements, saving the country perhaps trillions of dollars in the long term while increasing the nation's intellectual base as well. But politics and special interests have a nasty way of muddling the quest for an optimal solution.

Tainter, along with Jared Diamond and others, has identified why certain societies survive while others fail. In a nutshell, less stratified civilizations, ones with fewer divisions, are more likely to join together to make the needed sacrifices that allow the society as a whole to continue. On the other hand, in more complex societies, those with considerable divisions between rulers and commoners, the vested interests of various groups tend to trump the interests of society as a whole, which frequently results in revolt and societal collapse.

We can sum up by saying that America's belief in the power and endless growth of technology is unremitting. Yet our path toward achieving this growth has been utterly muddled by our faith in the computer and the Internet. Our chances for a major breakthrough are therefore minimal. One urgent message is that if by chance we do achieve a major technological achievement that brings alternative energies into view, let's keep it to ourselves until we are absolutely sure that sharing it in no way compromises our ability to use it.

No Substitute for Creativity

Perhaps the most attentive audience your senior author has had in discussing the limitations of computers when it came to solving problems were several executives of China's Sovereign Wealth Fund. They even listened when they were congratulated on their recent successes in the chess world. No proprietary secret was shed when they were told that to make it to the top slot they would have to use computers as a tool for problem-solving rather than as a problem-solver in and of itself. To wit:

When the IBM computer dubbed Big Blue beat world champion Garry Kasparov in a ballyhooed 1997 chess match, the case for computer or artificial intelligence was given a tremendous boost. Man had been bested in a game that for centuries had been considered as requiring the ultimate in intellectual ability.

Or was there another explanation? In our book *Defying the Market* we analyzed the match, concluding that it was much more a case of man beating man—that is, of Kasparov beating himself—than of machine beating man. Kasparov resigned a game that was actually a draw, because he became psychologically stunned when the computer varied moves from one game to the next. (The reason was that one of the programmers had made a program adjustment.) By the last and deciding game, Kasparov was psychologically drained and lost in an opening variation that most good teenage chess players wouldn't play.

What was really remarkable about the match was how readily the press jumped on the bandwagon. It was almost universally accepted that computer intelligence had trumped human brainpower.

Still, we have to give chess computers their due—they do play chess at an extremely high level. But do computers play or do they simply follow human instructions? All evidence points to the latter. What programmers have done is to reduce chess to a game in which computers only have to make computations. Roughly speaking, using the judgments of the best chess masters, positions are assigned a value. By raw calculating skills computers are capable of assigning values for positions perhaps six or seven moves into the future. Humans cannot calculate that far.

But the humans who do the chess programming are not necessarily the best chess players. Or more precisely, it is not always true that the algorithms they've developed to assess the strength of various positions have taken everything possible into account. That's because some players use a set of valuations different from those considered standard. One such player is the extraordinarily gifted Ukrainian Vassily Ivanchuk. Born in a small village, Ivanchuk learned chess through a motley combination of reading, playing, and thinking. When he was a youth, no coach was available, so he was never inculcated with the accepted chess canon. When he plays at his best, his games are extraordinary on many levels. Very often he goes for positions that can't be evaluated by even the strongest grandmasters, nor—and this is the key point—by computers. The games can be nightmares for chess coaches, as he makes moves that turn out to be winning ones, only no one else understands why.

The point is that if you can transform chess into a series of calculations, humans will be at a disadvantage. But even here much of the disadvantage is psychological as well as a matter of time. If you give some humans enough time, they are likely to more than equal the computer. But when humans play outside the "book" used to program computers, the computers don't do very well. For Ivanchuk, playing outside the book is natural, and he usually doesn't need extra time. For other elite grandmasters, playing outside the book would require extra time but they could probably do it. What it comes down to is that computers totally lack anything resembling creative skills— they are incredible calculating machines, but nothing more.

Chapter 9

The Limits of Western Democracy in Dealing with Critical Problems: Tiananmen Square versus 9/11

For most of the twentieth century the United States was, by many measures, the greatest nation the world had ever known. But in this century, some of our greatest virtues have become weaknesses, especially when compared to China, an autocratic culture with more than two millennia of history.

It's not accidental that at times in the twentieth century the United States was able to succeed because it knew when to put its great virtues on hold. During World War II, for instance, though far from a dictatorship, the country became more autocratic while remaining united and resourceful. As Martin Jacques, author of *When China Rules the World: The Rise of the Middle Kingdom and the End of the Western World*, points out, democracy in the United States has always been more limited than we think. During the country's greatest period of growth, in the latter part of the nineteenth century, only a small portion of the population voted. Indeed, with the possible exception of India, most countries that have made tremendous economic strides have done so when they were at best only partial democracies. The point is that a democratic system of government is neither necessary nor sufficient for strong economic growth.

Since their embrace of capitalism, the Chinese have had a major advantage over the United States: They have been able to focus their sights almost monomaniacally on growth, while we, for the most part satiated on material well-being, have had much more diffuse ambitions. We took our basic freedoms for granted and indeed considered it a mission to spread our democratic way of life across the globe. Our military might was unsurpassed and we felt safe and secure. Perhaps most relevant, the United States has never fought a war for want of something. All our wars have been fought in the name of freedom and American values, not because we needed resources.

The events of September 11, 2001, should have changed our view. We should have seen it as evidence of impending resource vulnerability. Instead, we went to war to defend our freedom from what turned out to be phantom threats—Saddam Hussein's putative weapons of mass destruction—and to attempt to bring our democratic principles into other parts of the world.

Doing this—as well as deciding to fight two wars at once—was tragically misguided. A few years before 9/11 we had read an interview with Arthur C. Clarke that really changed how we look at the world. Clarke, who was by no means a pessimist, noted that the period directly ahead was likely to be the most challenging in the history of humankind. He specified four problems that were rapidly converging: the environment, energy, population, and nuclear proliferation.

The implication was clear: Solve energy and you solve everything. Abundant energy would mean plentiful freshwater by virtue of desalinization. Renewable energies would solve the environment problem. As for nuclear proliferation, consider that the countries that most concern us are those that can hold us ransom to our need for oil. Most of the terrorists who participated in the 9/11 attacks were Saudi nationals. Clearly, if the Muslim world did not have such an economic stranglehold on us, it would be much easier to conduct the kind of surveillance (and perhaps more aggressive actions) that sharply limit the potential for nuclear proliferation. Think: If Iran did not have oil as a weapon, there would be little stopping us from eliminating their nuclear processing facilities.

The attacks of 9/11 offered us a catalyst to tackle and solve the energy problem. The proper fight at that time would have been to wage war against our dependence on fossil fuels rather than one that may have promised to extend the life of fossil fuels. But Richard Nisbett and other psychologists have made it clear that the Western perspective is almost always to look at the center of the picture. And at the center of 9/11 was an attack on the United States, which required a direct, in-kind response.

As mentioned earlier but is worth repeating again: Nobel Prize–winning economist Joseph Stiglitz estimates we've spent $3 trillion so far on the wars in Iraq and Afghanistan. It is tragic to think that if we had spent that sum on developing alternative energies instead, the United States would be positioned to extend its hegemony well into the twenty-first century. For example, as we said above, Iran's development of nuclear weapons could be shut down immediately if it weren't for the fear that the Iranians, by shutting down the Strait of Hormuz, could cut off our economic lifeblood— oil. Environmental problems could have been solved, and with nearly unlimited supplies of renewable energies, America would have been positioned to lead the world for at least another century and probably much longer.

Smashing the Iron Rice Bowl

In a way, China's leaders have operated in a constant state of crisis since Chairman Deng Xiaoping began reforms in 1978 in an attempt to balance the need for increasing prosperity while maintaining the Chinese Communist Party's grip on power. And they've been quite successful in adapting to meet these twin endeavors. One major threat they've had to contend with, while not directly comparable to the attacks on 9/11, still serves to contrast how the Chinese and Americans respond to crises, and how they are better prepared to deal with resource scarcity. First a little history.

In 1978 Deng launched what he termed a "second revolution" to open and revitalize the Chinese economy. What followed has been more than thirty years in which China's growth has on average exceeded 10 percent annually. China's economic reforms during this time have moved through several gradual yet distinct phases, each geared toward raising living standards but also designed to preserve the party's power. The cautious pace of these reforms has been and will likely continue to be best characterized by Deng's phrase of "feeling for rocks while crossing the river"—an endeavor best conducted in a slow, deliberate manner.

Initially, a nearly completely planned economy gave way to central planning supplemented by market incentives and some personal freedoms that went along with those incentives. The country's agricultural sector was the first to benefit; collective farms were decentralized and granted the autonomy to decide which crops to grow and trade fair restrictions were removed. Enterprises were allowed to retain a portion of their profits for the first time.

To attract foreign investment and technology, and to promote exports, special economic zones were created along China's east coast. Manufacturers took advantage of low-cost labor and tax breaks, while previously underemployed migrant laborers found work. Collective farms were broken up and individuals were encouraged to take up entrepreneurial enterprises without fear of being denounced or imprisoned as "capitalist roaders." Opposition to these reforms within the conservative ranks of the Communist Party was considerable, but still the "to get rich is glorious" sentiment prevailed.

About five years after China began moving away from total state control of the economy toward free-market principles, the country—led by sharp gains in the rural economy—enjoyed its fastest growth in the communist era. But it was believed that achieving further success would require what Deng called "smashing the iron rice bowl."

After 1984 the government wanted to expand its reforms to the urban population. The leadership broadened the scope of reform, moving closer to allowing the market to regulate the prices consumers paid. It set quotas and purchased manufactured goods at fixed prices; anything produced above quota could then be sold on the open market.

This turned out to be a recipe for near disaster that led to massive inflation and rampant corruption. The big problem was that the vast majority of companies controlling production were state-owned firms. The dual pricing gave them tremendous economic power, at the expense of private enterprise. Social inequalities widened, and though growth continued, the country had clearly taken several steps backward.

In mid-1988 the state tried to assuage the situation by eliminating dual pricing in favor of market pricing. As Wang Hui, author of *The End of the Revolution*, put it, "This, however, led to panic purchasing and large-scale social instability." He added, "Even as this period of reform had a number of successes, it also produced certain new conditions that, in different ways, reflected new social inequalities. These became motivating factors for the eruption of the 1989 social movement."

The partial decentralization of state-owned enterprises and the introduction of private enterprise brought with it mass layoffs and rising inequalities. While many enjoyed a rising standard of living, many more Chinese felt the sting of declining socioeconomic mobility. Growth continued at a rapid pace, but it was accompanied by soaring unemployment and a rapidly increasing cost of living. Inflation rose from around 5 percent when Deng began to liberalize the economy to more than 25 percent in the spring of 1989. This upheaval gave birth to a protest movement that would reach its apex in Beijing's Tiananmen Square.

Today, more than twenty years after the fact, Western media tend to frame the Tiananmen Square protests that arose during this second phase of reforms simply in terms of a student-led democracy movement. After all, the students rallied around a Liberty-like thirty-three-foot Goddess of Democracy statue they erected in the square. In actuality, people were drawn to the protest movement for many reasons, mostly having nothing to do with a desire to set up a democratic form of administration. It was the government's social and economic policies—as well as discontent with the widespread corruption that had emerged alongside economic reform—more than a desire to elect government representatives that prompted people to take to the streets.

It was an open secret that high-ranking party members and their family members were disproportionately benefiting from the reforms, even as many workers found themselves unemployed now that unprofitable enterprises were laying off workers (a previously unheard-of event in the country). Others, including many intellectuals, though still employed, suffered from a declining standard of living as wages remained largely static even as inflation raged. The state was seen as not fulfilling its traditional role.

Concurrently, students were seeking greater personal freedom. At the time, the state-run universities exerted considerable control over their student bodies, a holdover from the Maoist era. Curfews and restrictions on dating were enforced, for instance. Freedom of expression was limited, as was the availability of popular books and music.

The death of Hu Yoabang in April 1989 set the wheels in motion for the Tiananmen Square protests. The former general secretary of the Communist Party, Hu had been ousted from his position due to his hard-line stance toward cleaning up corruption. Students and workers alike essentially saw in Hu's passing the death of a martyr. An estimated 100,000 people turned out in Tiananmen Square for his funeral, but the mourning quickly morphed into a mass protest demanding political reform.

Tiananmen is the largest public square in the world, capable of accommodating a million people. The square had been the site of protests in the past and it held a significant position in the history of the creation of the Communist Party, a fact not lost on either the protestors or the ruling elite. In 1919 students gathered in Tiananmen Square to pro est the government's acceptance of the Treaty of Versailles. The treaty, which formally ended World War I, was seen by those protestors as being unfair to China. Those demonstrations spread to Shanghai and what became known as the May Fourth movement, which ultimately led to the genesis of China's Communist Party.

Though Tiananmen Square became shorthand in the West for the protests and crackdown that followed, the demonstrations reached far beyond the Beijing public square and were actually carried out across the country. In China today, the events of 1989 are simply referred to as "June 4" or "the unfortunate incident."

As the crowd swelled in Tiananmen and protests gained momentum in other cities, it was becoming clear that this was the greatest threat to its existence the Communist Party had ever encountered. Three months before the students and workers staged their sit-in at Tiananmen, Deng Xiaoping, although the champion of reform, voiced his concern about the protest movement, stating, "China cannot allow demonstrations to happen too easily . . . or else foreign investment will stop flowing in." Deng recognized the protest movement as a threat to both the supremacy of the Communist Party and continued economic reform.

Communist Europe was also under attack from internal dissenters at this time. Like Deng, Mikhail Gorbachev was steering the Soviet Union toward openness (glasnost) and economic restructuring (perestroika) in an attempt to preserve his Communist Party's preeminence. Gorbachev's planned visit to Beijing in May 1989 served to spark calls from Chinese students and intellectuals for even greater freedoms. The growing protest movement resonated with workers who, as we said, had their own grievances with the state.

Hoping to bring a swift end to the rebellion, Deng imposed martial law days after Gorbachev's visit, putting troops on the ground. But that decision only stiffened the resolve of the protestors. The world was captivated by video footage of a nameless student, grocery bags in hand, blocking a column of tanks that was attempting to move on the people gathered in the square.

In the early hours of June 4, the troops did move in. It's estimated that more than eight hundred people were gunned down in the army action. Further uprisings were squelched through repression, including the arrests of tens of thousands.

The government crackdown led to a brief halt in market reforms and the most liberal of the reform-minded members were purged from the party's ranks. But the CCP did not retreat altogether from its effort to transform the economy. Martial law was lifted in January 1990. People still had the opportunity to generate and keep the profits from their labor. And in addition to being allowed to pursue their material well-being, the Chinese people were also permitted personal freedoms formerly out of reach—in exchange for not questioning the CCP's ultimate authority.

The government also took steps to rein in the overheating economy. A year after the Tiananmen uprising those efforts were bearing fruit. GDP was still expanding at a healthy, double-digit pace and inflation had dropped to less than 3 percent.

The demise of Communist Party rule in the Soviet Union in 1991 opened up the next opportunity to further restructure China's economy. The leadership realized that the party's legitimacy and continued existence would rest on sustained economic growth. Equally important, Deng and other members of China's ruling body realized that they still had the freedom to continue to implement the reforms that had started in 1979. As Martin Jacques puts it, "One of the most fundamental features of Chinese politics concerns the overriding emphasis placed on the country's unity. . . . The fact that China has spent so much of its history in varying degrees of disunity, and at such great cost, has taught the Chinese that unity is sacrosanct."

Not surprisingly, in surveys the Chinese consistently rank stability as far more important than do people from other countries. The breakup of the Soviet Union thus gave China's leaders great scope in furthering reforms, when ironically virtually the entire world expected China to revert to Maoist authoritarianism.

We are not saying that it was smooth sailing in the wake of the uprising in 1989. There were many deaths as a result of martial law and many intellectuals were jailed. But one story worth repeating on the country's overriding desire for unity was reported by James Kynge in his book *China Shakes the World*. Cao Siyuan was widely recognized prior to 1989 as a brilliant and forceful advocate of economic reforms. He was widely credited with drafting a bankruptcy code, which according to Kynge earned Cao the sobriquet "Mr. Bankruptcy." Following the uprising in 1989, Cao was imprisoned for a year—probably more because of his reputation as reformist and closeness to the "wrong" politicians than for any direct role he played.

You might expect that when Cao was released he would have been at least somewhat embittered. Quite the contrary. He became more determined than ever to promote the reforms he saw as necessary for the Chinese economy to succeed. Kynge quotes Cao as saying, "Often when I am making speeches, people ask me . . . will the central government be able to accept your points of view? I say . . . 'What is the central government? They are servants. They are servants of the people.'" At least in the eyes of Cao, state sovereignty and popular sovereignty did not have to be diametric opposites.

The story continues. In 1999 China was suffering as a result of the Asian crisis (though not nearly as much as other countries). Cao had occasion to attend a conference in which Chinese president Jiang Zemin was sitting in the front row. Jiang had been traveling the country maintaining that the state would never back the privatization of public enterprises. Cao had written a book arguing that exactly the opposite would be necessary for continued economic growth in China. At the conference he handed the book to Jiang, who accepted it without comment. Whether the book had an effect on the Chinese economy is anyone's guess. But the story clearly calls into question a stark contrast between state and popular control.

In January 1992 Deng embarked on a three-week tour of southern China, inspecting factories and visiting enterprises in Shenzhen and other special economic zones (SEZs), which he used to reignite market-oriented reform efforts, calling for an acceleration of growth and a further opening up to foreign investment. These policies were endorsed by the Politburo soon after. Additional SEZs were established and the privatization of state-owned enterprises (SOEs) accelerated.

Still, the gradualist nature of this reform was underscored by statements Deng made on the tour: "The reform and opening must continue to be discussed; the Party will have to go on discussing it for several decades. There will be differing opinions, but that too is out of good intentions. First, people are unaccustomed [to reform and opening]. Second, they're afraid, afraid problems will occur. For me alone to speak is not enough. Our party will have to speak, speak about it for several decades."

Deng clearly understood the entire mosaic that led up to 1989, and more than that he knew the right recipe for correcting those problems. Modifications were necessary—but economic growth had to continue. Moreover, if growth continued at a moderate rate the state was in no danger of losing its grip on broad decision-making. Again, this understanding of the entire situation was in stark contrast to what the West thought.

Under this "socialist market economy," still in effect today, power in many ways was shifted away from the central government in Beijing in favor of provincial and prefecture governments. Price controls were lifted and SOEs were allowed to decide what to produce and how to market their products. SOEs could also hire and fire workers at will. At the same time, inefficient firms that were unable to successfully cope in this new environment were increasingly likely to be shut down, although in practice subsidies and bailouts for many unprofitable SOEs continued for many years so as to prevent social and political upheaval.

Stock exchanges were established in Shanghai and Shenzhen to facilitate raising capital. The banking sector was also developed, including the creation of banks for the purpose of supporting industry, agriculture, and infrastructure, all essential to the nation's economic well-being.

Jiang Zemin replaced Deng as the country's supreme leader in 1997, carrying on Deng's reform legacy, including broadening legal rights in China, an essential step for joining the World Trade Organization. And in a bid to curb corruption, for the first time ever party members were subject to law, regardless of rank or status.

On the political front the country has liberalized to a degree, too. Direct elections of villagers' committees, which began prior to Tiananmen Square, were expanded and now occur throughout the country. These village committees are responsible for the administrative affairs in the villages, such as financial management, housing, education, and dispute resolution.

Power at the top echelons of government also became somewhat less centralized. Members of the People's Congress would have to stand for election, rather than simply be appointed. Congress no longer merely rubber-stamped the Politburo's decisions. Policy issues were more likely to be debated and voted upon rather than instituted by decree from the top, in what can be thought of as interparty democracy. The judiciary was also strengthened and laws enacted to increase transparency.

But like Deng, Jiang often underscored the importance of maintaining peace and stability—shorthand for the government not tolerating dissent. In one speech that emphasized this view, Jiang said, "The broad masses of the people [would work] under the leadership of the Party and in accordance with the Constitution."

Under Jiang, private and foreign-invested enterprises comprised a growing proportion of the nation's output. Import restrictions and licensing requirements were lifted and customs tariffs were reduced. The preferential policies governing SEZs were extended to all provincial capitals and a number of border cities.

In Jiang's footsteps, Hu Jintao has carried on this legacy, opening the economy to more laissez-faire policies. These policies have been an unqualified success, as the country has been a magnet for foreign investment. Cheap labor and favorable tax policies have made it an ideal place for manufacturers to set up shop. The focus has primarily been on manufacturing low-cost, export-oriented goods, but foreign investors have also long coveted selling products to the hundreds of millions of Chinese who are being lifted out of extreme poverty thanks to the unparalleled growth the country has enjoyed in the last several decades.

Along with foreign capital and the millions of jobs that have been created, China has benefited from the importation of management practices as well as important technology, either willingly shared by foreign partners looking to bolster their foothold in the country, reverse engineered, or simply stolen in the theft of intellectual property, often done with the tacit approval of the Chinese government.

An example of the CCP's doctrine of absorbing foreign technology by any and all means was laid out in a 2006 Shanghai government article, "Suggestions on Further Strengthening the Work of Energy Conservation." The document offered goals that included "strengthening efforts to break bottlenecks in energy conservation science and technology. Competent administrative departments of science and technology at all levels shall give priority to the independent research and development, *import, assimilation and re-innovation* of energy conservation technologies, renewable energy resources and new energy resources as the focus of government input in science and technology and their efforts to promote the industrialization of high- and neo-technologies." (Italics added.)

Many of China's largest companies were founded and are controlled by current and former high-ranking government officials who know very well the party line on technology. Consider Huawei Technologies, which was founded by Ren Zhengfei, a former People's Liberation Army officer and a current Communist Party member. In a few short years' time, Huawei Technologies went from being a tiny reseller of imported telecom equipment for the Chinese domestic market to a major international manufacturer of wireless phone and networking equipment.

It's widely acknowledged that Huawei was able to make this transition on the illicit acquisition of technology from its rivals. For instance, Cisco Systems, the world's largest maker of networking equipment, sued Huawei after it discovered that the Chinese company copied not only the software code used in its routers, the machines that connect online networks, but also Cisco's user interface, its model numbers, and user manuals—making it easier for customers to switch to the cheaper Huawei versions of the equipment. The theft was so blatant that a Huawei user manual contained the same spelling errors found in Cisco's manual for the same product.

Cisco ultimately dropped the suit after Huawei yanked the disputed products from the market and agreed to alter its software codes. Neither company would reveal greater details about the settlement, but we suspect Cisco's decision to settle such an important threat to its business had more than a little to do with its desire for access to the potentially lucrative Chinese market.

China continues to increase its research and development capacity in no small part with the aid of international partners. Intel, DuPont, Applied Materials . . . numerous leading-edge U.S. technology companies are conducting R&D work in China, where land and labor costs are low and the government offers generous tax incentives. Many of these companies recognize that at some point their intellectual property will eventually fall into Chinese hands, either through technology transfers, reverse engineering, or outright theft. But although operating in China puts their intellectual property at risk in the long term, the general sentiment of most companies is that they can't afford to forgo the short-run profits of being in China.

Achieving a State of Orderliness

Although the country's GDP has risen more than tenfold since 1978, China's gains have been far from uniform. Cities along the coast that were the earliest beneficiaries of the country's open door policy have enjoyed annual GDP growth far in excess of the nation as a whole. But for the 900 million still living in the countryside the gains have been far more muted.

In 2009 the income gap between rural and urban residents grew to its widest point since reforms began in 1978. And the problem is more than just an income gap; there are also quality-of-life issues that haven't been fully addressed. There are disparities in longevity, for instance, as rural residents are more likely to engage in high-risk behaviors and their access to health care is more limited. Urban dwellers typically have access to better housing and education than their rural counterparts. Even the availably of clean water can be an issue for many rural residents.

Placating these rural peasants, the traditional power base of the party, is essential to maintaining the legitimacy of the CCP. But the government has recognized that if it is to succeed with its aims, it must avoid the pitfalls that have befallen most other developing nations, including mass migration to cities leading to the creation of countless slums where chronic unemployment could ferment revolution. China's government obviously wants to move many of its rural residents to urban centers where it can better provide them with social services, but it wants to do this on its own timetable.

To do this the government has long relied on legal mechanisms to control the flow of its population to the cities. Resident permit laws known as the hukou system strictly limit the number of workers who can legally move from one area to another, forcing the estimated 150 million to 200 million migrants who have left the farms for the cities in search of work and higher wages to live in company dormitories. The hukou laws also prevent these workers from bringing their families along, since kids can't be enrolled in schools and access to health care and other social services is not available to them outside of their legal area of residence.

So while the invisible hand is increasingly at work in modern-day China's economy, the government's iron fist is still very much present. More blatant examples of this, familiar to most Westerners, are the country's oftentimes heavy-handed rule of Tibet and Xinjiang, China's westernmost provinces.

Despite the incremental moves toward social liberalization that have cropped up in recent years (the media now report on Politburo meetings, for instance), journalists are only allowed to question the CCP up to a point. Stories or op-ed pieces centered on human rights, Falun Gong (the outlawed religious movement), the Tiananmen Square massacre, holding free elections, and certain other topics are strictly forbidden. But as long as people are allowed the opportunity to increase their material well-being, they willingly accept the censorship and other social controls that are a part of their daily lives.

No doubt the Nobel Committee's decision to award the 2010 Peace Prize to jailed Chinese dissident Liu Xiaobo (who was one year into serving an eleven-year sentence for repeated human rights activism) was meant as a signal from the West that China should move forward with democratic reforms—much the same way the Peace Prize went to Burma's Aung San Suu Kyi in 1991. But if anything, the recipient choice will do nothing but solidify Beijing's stance on political reform occurring only slowly, on the CCP's timetable.

Besides, the vast majority of Chinese think the national government is doing a fairly good job. Their ire, if they do have problems, is largely directed at the local government level. In a 2008 poll conducted in nineteen countries, WorldPublicOpinion.org found that 83 percent of the Chinese people surveyed agreed that "government leaders should be selected through elections in which all citizens can vote." But when asked in the same survey how much their country was currently governed according to the "will of the people," no public scored their nation higher than the Chinese. In other words, despite living under an authoritarian system, the Chinese are largely content with their current form of government.

The global financial crisis reinforced for the Chinese people a general feeling that the country's economic system is thriving while the Western free-market system is on the wane. In a similar vein to the WorldPublic Opinion.org poll, Chinese respondents to an annual survey for the Pew Global Attitudes Project routinely indicate that they have a favorable view of the way things are going in their country—87 percent in 2009. In the United States that figure was 36 percent (up from just 23 percent in 2008).

In a similar vein, in 2004 Harvard sociologist Martin King Whyte undertook the first systematic nationwide survey of Chinese citizens to uncover how they felt about the inequalities that have resulted since China's economic reforms began in 1978. The results, published in his book *Myth of the Social Volcano: Perceptions of Inequality and Distributive Injustice in Contemporary China*, fly in the face of conventional Western perceptions.

Whyte found that despite considerable inequalities within Chinese society, most of the country's citizens, including the poorest rural peasants, are not dissatisfied with the current political system. Much like our own American dream, China's citizens see that talent and hard work can substantially improve their lot in life. Also, even though the market-based

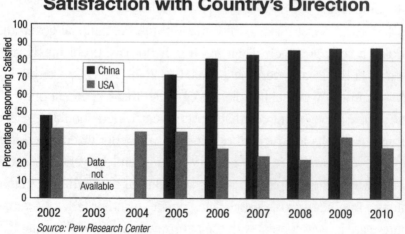

Satisfaction with Country's Direction

Source: Pew Research Center

economy has created greater inequalities today than under the old social-ist distribution system, Whyte's survey suggests that there is not an immi-nent threat of major social unrest in China based on perceptions that the system is unfair and corrupt. As long as people perceive that their stan-dard of living has risen and will continue to do so in the future, they are likely to remain content with the status quo.

Keep in mind that unlike the autocratic regimes of North Africa and the Middle East today, or of many Western governments for that matter, China has made actively addressing the inequalities that exist in its society a major component of its current Five-Year Plan for Economic and Social Development. This is more than mere lip service designed to appease its citizens. In 2010, for instance, wages for rural residents rose 11 percent, helping to narrow the income disparity with urban dwellers. Coupled with continued economic growth, the country's population will have even less reason to rise up against the leadership in Beijing.

Indeed, nationalism is replacing communism as China's chief ideol-ogy. Suisheng Zhao, executive director of the Center for China-U.S. Coop-eration and professor at the University of Denver's Graduate School of International Studies, writing in the *Journal of Contemporary China*, has made the case that "to an extent, it may be argued that the role of the communist state has reverted back to that of the traditional and highly ritualized Confucian state, particularly at the grass-roots levels."

The country also has a bureaucratic tradition that stretches back thousands of years. So long as the government stands up to its end of the bargain, its people are not likely to demand a significant change in the status quo.

The Chinese government has proven repeatedly that it is capable of completing big projects in a hurry. Stories of highways cropping up seem-ingly overnight or vast tracts of high-rise apartments appearing where rice paddies recently stood are commonplace. New airports, universities, and other infrastructure emblematic of a prosperous developing nation have also radically altered the nation's landscape in recent years. During the next decade, the most impressive public works projects in China will be its unprecedented construction of alternative power generation capacity.

Though the parallels may be far from perfect, it is worth comparing our response to 9/11 with the Chinese response to Tiananmen Square. While the Chinese recognized that the continuation of reforms, albeit at a moderate pace, would be the right medicine for assuring that dissent was kept under control and that the populace would continue to experience a better life, the United States paid only passing attention to what its real problems were in 2001. We remember writing a piece in one of our newsletters saying that despite the horror of 9/11 there were reasons for optimism. The United States finally had a mandate for attacking the underlying problems that could ultimately threaten our civilization.

Maybe it is too soon to make an historical judgment, but it seems clear that had we followed another path in the period after 9/11, our lifestyle and, more important, the lifestyle we can expect for our children would be much greater today than it is.

We love the American way of life. But it seems clear that America's tendency to focus on immediacy and fixate on the "center of the picture" has its drawbacks in dealing with a world that requires the recognition of nuances about background conditions and long-term planning. One criticism we expect to hear with this book is that we are giving the Chinese leadership too much credit, that despite the findings of Nisbett and others there is no question that even with their advantages of time perspective and their broader overall perspective, the Chinese can make mistakes.

Still, we are haunted by the words of widely respected British historian E. M. Gombrich. In *A Little History of the World*, Gombrich comments that "China is, in fact, the only country in the world to be ruled for hundreds of years, not by nobility, nor by soldiers, nor even by the priesthood, but by scholars. No matter where you came from, or whether you were rich or poor, as long as you gained high marks in your exams you could become an official. The highest post went to the person with the highest marks." China's leaders are every bit up to the trial at hand, and they have actively embarked on a course to confront the biggest threat the modern world has encountered.

James Schlesinger, who served as the first U.S. energy secretary, once remarked that Americans have only two ways of thinking about energy: "complacency and panic." All signs suggest that America is facing challenges of a sort we have never seen before. And as a result of our form of government, run by politicians who are constantly focused on the next election and who unswervingly choose political expediency rather than tackling difficult tasks of addressing the long-term needs of the nation, we are complacently rushing headlong toward a crisis of epic proportions. We must set aside politics and act as well, before it's too late and panic sets in.

Chapter 10

Responses to the Financial Crisis of 2008

In the previous chapter we detailed how dissimilarities in mindsets and perspectives created huge differences between China and the United States in how they responded to major crises—Tiananmen Square for the Chinese and 9/11 for America. Here we move to 2008 and again compare differing responses to what many have called the greatest threat to capitalism: the economic crisis precipitated by the housing bubble and surging commodity prices. The differences in response were strongly formed by how the countries had managed their economies in the decade leading up to 2008. They also demonstrate how China is so much better prepared than the United States for the impending resource contest.

In 1998 the world faced another period of extreme financial turmoil. The rising value of the U.S. dollar of the previous several years was taking its toll on the export-oriented economies of Southeast Asia, which had pegged their currencies to the greenback. The so-called Asian Tigers—named for the dynamic growth their economies had enjoyed throughout the decade—were feeling the pinch of worsening current account deficits as their exports were becoming increasingly less competitive. This was a result of both the rising value of the dollar and China's growing presence in world trade.

In July 1997 the debt-saddled government of Thailand threw in the towel and allowed its previously pegged currency, the baht, to float relative to the dollar. Removing the peg prompted a pronounced outflow of foreign capital and in the next several months the baht lost more than half its value while the Thai stock market sank 75 percent. Worse still, Thailand's misery had a cascading effect across the region in the subsequent months.

As the contagion spread, most Asian currencies, stock markets, and economies collapsed, though China, the largest emerging market economy in the region, was relatively unaffected. China's financial markets had the benefit of being less evolved than those of its neighbors. They had not been inappropriately liberalized, which economists Graciela Kaminsky and Carmen Reinhart have argued typically precede a currency crisis. China relied less on debt to fund its growth, and complex derivative instruments had yet to be introduced there. Likewise, the sharp drop in the fledgling Shanghai stock market did not have an adverse impact on the economy because few Chinese were active investors at the time. Notorious savers—in part due to the country's inadequate social safety net—the Chinese instead preferred to place their household wealth in old-fashioned savings accounts or under their mattresses. So what was a yawning ditch for most countries in Southeast Asia proved to be a mere pothole for China.

Soon other emerging economies around the globe were affected, however. The economic slowdowns caused commodity prices to fall sharply, led by a plunge in crude oil prices, which by 1998 were cut in half to less than $10 a barrel. That, along with a catastrophic decline in the ruble, forced the Russian government to suspend payments on its debt.

Much of the world was already in shambles when it was hit by a coup de grâce. The tumbling of emerging market currencies led to the collapse of the highly leveraged Long-Term Capital Management (LTCM), which had bet heavily on Russian bond prices recovering.

A Greenwich, Connecticut, hedge fund, LTCM was captained by the best and brightest in financial engineering. Its founder, John Meriwether, was the former vice chairman and head of bond trading at Salomon Brothers at a time when that firm was the dominant player in the bond market. Meriwether and his fellow Salomon bond traders were the inspiration for the Wall Street "Masters of the Universe" in Tom Wolfe's fictional tale *The Bonfire of the Vanities*. Meriwether was also feted in Michael Lewis' wildly entertaining book *Liar's Poker*.

Joining Meriwether's shop was David Mullins Jr., a former vice chairman of the Federal Reserve, and leading economists Myron Scholes and Robert Merton. The latter pair's fame would be sealed in 1997 when they would win the Nobel Prize in Economics for their pioneering work in valuing stock options. Their methodology led to more efficient risk management tools and gave birth to numerous types of financial instruments. *BusinessWeek* called the firm the "Dream Team" of high-tech traders, who relied heavily on computers to make trillions of calculations in miniscule time frames as a basis for investment decisions.

LTCM's investment approach was to seek out small but profitable opportunities in what were normally low-risk arbitrage trades that others had overlooked. They got off to a tremendous start, racking up annual returns in excess of 40 percent for their investors in the first two years of operations. It turned out, however, that the firm's highly sophisticated mathematical models, which worked exceedingly well in the fund's early years, did not allow for the extraordinary currency fluctuations that occurred in 1998.

Exacerbating the problem, though the fund was relatively small by Wall Street standards—a few billion dollars in assets—it used enormous leverage, borrowing around $125 billion and investing those funds in derivative positions such as interest rate swaps and long-term options with a notional value approaching $1.25 trillion. LTCM was so leveraged that the fund's failure threatened a domino effect in which the creditors most on the line would also fail and that, in turn, would lead to failures in other creditors. Some argued—probably rightfully so—that the entire financial system was tottering due to the misplaced bets of the relatively small hedge fund.

Alan Greenspan—now vilified for the happenings that fostered the 2008 financial crisis—was then lionized for the role he played in pulling the economy out of its tailspin. Not only did he help engineer a rescue of LTCM by the fund's largest creditors, but he also dramatically reversed monetary course from a tightening posture to loosening, lowering the federal funds rate three times in short order to spur the economy. The U.S. economy responded favorably to the moves, with consumers soon returning to their spendthrift ways. Economies around the world likewise stabilized, Asia being helped by the U.S. consumer's increased purchases and the Russian economy benefiting from peppier demand for commodities from the United States and Asia alike.

One lesson supposedly learned from the LTCM collapse is that financial models have a great deal of trouble accounting for extreme occurrences, sometimes referred to as "six sigma events" because they fall so far outside of the standard deviation of normal distribution assumptions. After all, LTCM had been doing extremely well until the dominoes started triggering events of catastrophic proportions that none of the models considered even remotely possible.

One example Roger Lowenstein pointed to in his book *When Genius Failed: The Rise and Fall of Long-Term Capital Management* was a wayward bet that LTCM took on the dual-listed shares of oil giant Royal Dutch Shell. The fund bought one stock and sold short the other in anticipation of the spread between the prices of the two narrowing. Instead, the spread widened from an already extremely wide 8 to 10 percent to an unheard-of premium of more than 20 percent—far above the range of what any model then thought possible. The adverse move by itself was bad enough, but it was greatly amplified by the use of leverage.

Some analysts, such as Nassim Taleb, author of the bestselling books *The Black Swan* and *Fooled by Randomness*, have argued that the underlying assumptions of many statistical models are flawed by failing to recognize the frequency of extreme occurrences. We, however, think it more educational to view extreme results as the failure of underlying assumptions that the majority have adopted. The British philosopher Bertrand Russell is well known for a quip in which he dared someone to make a false assumption (or axiom) and promised that he would then prove that he (an avowed atheist) and the pope were one. The party to the trick immediately replied that one plus one is one, to which Russell replied, "I am one, the pope is one, and therefore, we are indeed one."

Our point is that you don't need high-level mathematics to see where LTCM went wrong. Indeed, it is probably true that any horrific miscalculation can be traced to an incorrect assumption or axiom. In the case of LTCM, the assumption that irrationality had well-defined limits proved wrong—in the short term—because of extreme events. But the more general lesson is that regardless of how powerful your computer, if you don't fully understand the underlying variables that define your world, the computer is useless. And in the case of LTCM, computer power was more than useless.

Lesson learned? Unfortunately not, at least for the United States.

Critical Assumptions in a Changing World

Between 1998 and 2008 the Chinese and American economies took vastly different courses. The Chinese continued to follow the same course that they did in the wake of Tiananmen Square—strong and steady growth was accompanied by ever greater privatization. Even companies controlled by the government, such as PetroChina, were allowed a great deal of freedom in managing their business. In the early part of the decade, super-investor Warren Buffett took a big stake in PetroChina, which was tantamount to a major endorsement of the public-private management that characterized a number of major Chinese companies. Buffett was not disappointed for taking this chance, as he made more than $2 billion on his shares.

China's growth concentrated on manufacturing and infrastructure. As a manufacturer, it was able to take advantage of its very low-cost labor and became the world's largest exporter. The country also spent immense sums on building out its infrastructure. One reason was to create a pathway between the massive poor rural population and the more affluent urbanites. There were other reasons for the country's massive infrastructure projects as well, but we will save those for a little later.

A consequence of China's growth, along with growth in other developing countries, was that the 2000s witnessed explosive gains in commodity prices. When most people think about the commodity boom of the last decade, oil is what comes to mind. And it's true that oil is in many ways the kingpin of commodities: The value of oil consumed is greater than that of any other commodity, and the value of oil traded is greater than that of any other commodity. So for many good reasons oil did capture most of the headlines. But it was not just oil that soared during the decade— virtually every other commodity took off as well. Iron ore prices, for example, marched almost in lockstep with oil. Copper, often viewed as a key leading economic indicator, climbed about sevenfold from its 2001 low to its high in 2008. And so it was with almost all commodities.

A point which we cannot stress strongly enough is that commodities are an interdependent mesh that cannot be disentangled from one another. If oil goes up, so does the cost of delivering iron ore, so too does the cost of mining copper, and so—in the self-reinforcing circle—does the price of finding more oil and other fossil fuels. It is true, as we pointed out in the last chapter, that if you solve "energy" you solve most other problems. But the crux of the matter is that to solve the energy problem you also have to solve the scarcity of many other commodities as well.

The run in commodities last decade was not accompanied by what you would have expected based on past history. In contrast to the 1970s when, despite two recessions, U.S. economic growth was on balance quite strong, growth was at best mediocre through 2008. And when you include the last two years of the decade, growth was the slowest since the Great Depression. Yet even after commodities fell sharply following the crisis in 2008, they were still the standout investment of the decade. This disparity between commodity prices and America's growth was unprecedented.

Also true is that surging commodity prices did not lead to sharply rising inflation in America—at least not until 2008, when headline inflation was flirting with 5 percent. The reason for the lack of growth and relatively low inflation was the same: The source of the gains in commodities did not come from America, but rather from surging growth in China and other developing countries. In effect, the United States no longer had control of its own economy. That control had passed to the developing world, whose growth was sharply constricting the availability of resources.

By way of analogy, consider two gardens, one tended by someone with a green thumb, the other by someone barely able to grow weeds. For the guy with the green thumb, higher fertilizer prices could actually be viewed as a sign of success. For the poor brown-thumbed gardener, however, those higher prices are nothing more than a confiscatory tax. And so it is with the United States vis-à-vis China and the developing world: Higher commodity prices have occurred because of China's strong demand for materials, whereas for the United States rising commodities have simply increased the cost of doing business, without a corresponding gain in GDP. Keep in mind, too, that if our poor brown-thumbed gardener is determined to maintain a certain lifestyle, his only choice is to borrow increasing amounts of money. Sound familiar?

In view of the deflationary impact that rising commodities prices were having on the economy, it is remarkable that only a month or so before the collapse of Lehman Brothers, which set the financial crisis in motion, the Fed was considering raising interest rates to keep inflation in check. Rising commodity prices, and in particular rising oil prices, are a brake on the U.S. economy. They were already slowing it down to such an extent that when Lehman went under we were more than six months into a recession, though the Business Cycle Dating Committee at the National Bureau of Economic Research had yet to make it official. Still, here was the Fed actually debating whether they should raise interest rates when the economy was in desperate need of lower rates to fight the recession. The message of a changing world had been completely missed by the Fed.

Not only had policymakers missed the macro message, but on a micro level they were unaware of the proverbial wrong assumption that so many Wall Street "quants" had also missed. The housing crisis has already been well documented, so we won't discuss it here. But we just can't resist pointing out that all the financial engineering, all the derivatives that went so awry, were designed with a critical assumption in mind—that housing prices, which in nominal terms had never declined in the postwar era, would not fall. As with LTCM, this again was a case of misplaced faith in computers. Financial instruments were created that no human being could fully understand other than to recognize (largely with the benefit of hindsight) that they were again based on false assumptions. It was computers running wild—without an understanding of the variables underlying the situation.

We admit that in 2007–08, we too did not believe home prices would fall markedly. We were certain—or as certain as you can be when it comes to things economic—that the Fed would do whatever it took to assure that prices remained on an even keel. When the Fed in effect blessed policies (steady interest rates in the face of rising commodities) that were de facto restrictive in 2008, we were sure they had the situation under control. Why were we so sure? Just take a look at a few quotes from a previous book, *The Coming Economic Collapse*, which was published in 2006:

> If home prices suddenly started to fall, the result would easily be the vicious circle to end all vicious circles. . . . Could the policymakers rescue such a situation? Clearly, it would be a far greater challenge than rescuing the economy in the wake of the tech bubble. It would take massive amounts of money. Interest rates would likely

fall to zero. Government spending would need to reach unimagin-
ably high levels. In other words, if the economy survived, it would
emerge with much higher debt levels than before. Moreover, we
would still face the same hideous inflationary problem, a shortage
of energy, and the prospect of sharply rising oil prices.

Our mistake was missing the fallibility of our economic policymakers. With the consequences of falling housing prices so grim, we never
dreamed that the critical decision-makers would let it happen. Lesson
learned in spades.

But there is no indication that policymakers have finally learned
that the real problems besieging and utterly threatening our way of life
revolve around commodities. America, unfortunately, acts as if it is still
not convinced that even oil is a strategic threat to its economy. And this
was compounded by the belief that the housing crisis would be confined
to so-called subprime mortgages. Yet the extraordinary complexity of the
instruments made it impossible for even the best on Wall Street to understand how intertwined all housing was with subprime housing.

If we look at how the Chinese reacted to the 2008 crisis, there is no
mistaking that they have become even more aware that resource scarcity
is, by a very wide margin, the most critical economic concern of our time.
And not only that, but the Chinese financial system was relatively simple
and direct; every action could be understood by any of the policymakers.
Computers were used as tools in China, not as creators of artificial wealth.
In other words, China's focus on the long-term health of its economy and
its unwillingness to yield control to computers assured that 2008 was an
opportunity rather than a catastrophe.

There is another point, too, that relates to computers and societal
well-being, in which China has a decided edge, and explains why it has
avoided financial catastrophes. Stock markets—indeed almost all financial
markets—are designed to allocate resources. When they lose their raison
d'être—when stocks are not priced according to their long-term prospects,

when bonds don't reflect underlying economic growth and inflation, or when commodities are not priced in a way to let producers hedge—serious problems occur.

In America toward the end of the last decade most markets became and continue today to function as casinos; an incalculable number of roulette wheels in which profits overwhelmingly accrue for those who run the games—Wall Street with their massive computers. By some counts, computer-driven trading comprises well over 50 percent of the daily volume on the New York Stock Exchange these days. High-frequency trading strategies (HFT), as they are known, are computerized trading activities that at the risk of oversimplifying take advantage of price differences that exist on the market for tiny fractions of a second. The programs rely on very complex algorithms to find opportunities. By buying and selling high volumes of shares rapidly, the computers generate profits for their operators.

The problem with HFT is that it creates no real wealth; instead it merely rewards people for cheating the system, without creating jobs or providing any benefit to the world. Worse, HFT harms society as a whole, by diverting money away from enterprises and individuals who would benefit the world—such as innovative scientists—and from investors. It also discourages the public from buying stocks, since average investors know they cannot compete against the computers. The more the market appears rigged, the more legitimate money migrates to the sidelines, and the harder it is for good businesses to raise capital.

By contrast, in China markets function as markets should: Their stock market is designed to raise money for deserving companies. Middlemen play a role, but they are wholly subordinate to the well-motivated buyers and sellers.

One other instructive lesson can be gleaned from the differences between China and the United States. For most of 2010, a group of American investors were waiting for an inevitable collapse in Chinese housing prices, which had been bid up to extremely high levels. But unlike in America, the housing boom there was not driven by wild leverage or financial instruments that no one, not even the designers, understood. As a result, the so-called Chinese housing bubble was tamed by highly focused government action rather than a collapse the Americans saw as inevitable. In America, focused intervention—even if the Fed had wanted to go down that path—was not possible in 2008, as everything was so tightly connected to everything else.

The Short and Long View

You don't get second chances very often. We certainly missed one chance to correct our energy problem in the wake of 9/11. And we again did not seize the opportunity when it occurred in the wake of the 2008 financial crisis.

The U.S. stimulus package, a bit less than $800 billion, was the initial legislation of a new president. The lofty goal was to create a bipartisan way of alleviating what was widely recognized as the worst economy since the Great Depression. Emphasis was placed on short-term gains and passing the package as expeditiously as possible. Drafting the plan was turned over to the House of Representatives. The result was a hodgepodge of different programs with very little focus on longer-term priorities. Despite the universally recognized economic crisis, the vote for the package was completely one-sided. Indeed, not one Republican supported a measure that many considered vital for America's economic survival.

Perhaps most disappointing was Congress deciding that almost any spending was good spending. The bulk of the allocated funds went to consumers and to projects designed to foster consumer spending. Long-term investments were a relatively minor portion of the package, with very little of the funds dedicated to solving our energy problem. No consideration was given to the fact that we had been through nearly a decade in which rising energy and commodity prices held back economic growth and were no doubt at least partially responsible for the tremendous buildup of debt in the economy. In our garden analogy above there was little doubt that the American consumer was not only cursed with a brown thumb but also was intent on experiencing an ever better lifestyle. Clearly, rising debt was the only solution.

According to most data, the stimulus package allocated about 12 percent to energy. Of that, the largest sum went to creating more energy-efficient buildings. We have no major quarrel with buildings that use less energy. But unfortunately, that does not point the way to an economy that is working toward independence of nonrenewable energies. The answer to our energy problem is not so much using less nonrenewable fuels but further developing renewable energies. In a world where energy consumption is rising, less consumption in the United States will only mean more consumption in other countries. Between 2000 and 2009, for instance, U.S. oil consumption had hardly grown, yet oil prices had climbed manifold on the back of rising consumption in China and other developing countries.

The Chinese stimulus package was dramatically different from our own spending plan in almost every aspect. For starters, it was much larger in relative terms. The Chinese package amounted to nearly 18 percent of that country's GDP, whereas the U.S. package was about 5 percent of the economy. The difference was magnified by the fact that the Chinese economy was in much better shape than that of the United States. The Chinese banking system, for instance, was much stronger than its U.S. counterpart and was able to continue to make new loans, whereas our banks reduced their loan portfolios in a bid to shore up their weakened balance sheets.

Besides the size of the packages, there were other glaring differences. The Chinese package allocated nearly 40 percent to the development of renewable energies. Excluding what the United States had allocated to energy efficiency, this meant in absolute terms that the Chinese planned to spend more than four times what the United States had designated for renewable energies. Maybe even more striking, though the Chinese economy represented only about 5 percent of the world's economy, their planned outlay on renewable energy accounted for more than 50 percent of total world stimulus spending in that category.

In the end, no one will be able to accurately tally what each country actually spent on what. In the United States what mattered was a short-term fix and political posturing. The Chinese approached their stimulus spending as much more than just a short-term necessity. Rather, their goal was to create the means for a cleaner, self-sustaining economy. Had they allocated as much to defense as they did to alternative energies, we think it nearly certain that America would have taken notice and responded in kind.

This brings us once again back to psychologist Richard Nisbett. Unless the war is directly in front of us, unless we can clearly and unmistakably identify the threat, we are unlikely to react. The Chinese, on the other hand, have identified a massive threat to their economy and are taking every step in their power to fight it.

Ironically, some analysts have argued that growth in China is much too heavily tilted toward investment and that as a result bubbles are nearly assured. These are bubbles beyond the property bubbles in some cities. They are bubbles that concern how much the country is investing in roads, steel mills, railways, urban centers, and the like. The argument is that there has never been a country in which investment spending has been such a high percentage of economic growth. And that is true if you count only peacetime economies. But the assertion is completely false if you look at, say, the United States during World War II, when investment spending was an even greater portion of GDP growth than it is in China today.

Our argument is that the need to switch from nonrenewable energies to renewable ones has to be treated on the same footing as a war in that the entire economy rests on whether we win or lose.

Chapter 11

The Other Critical Metal: Gold

It is not just metals and minerals related to energy production that interest the Chinese. Based on the actions of the People's Bank of China (BOC), and the country's annual mining output relative to its reserves, gold is arguably the metal the Chinese covet most of all.

Despite some mixed messages in which BOC officials have said that gold is a good but not a great investment, it seems clear that China wants to accumulate as much gold as possible and as quickly as possible. For example, at the end of 2009 a few bank officials were arguing that the gold market was too volatile and too small to be a large part of their reserves, then valued at $2.4 trillion. At the same time, Ji Xiaonan, a leading official who plays a major role in regulating state-owned enterprises, was quoted in the Chinese press as saying that within three to five years China's gold reserve should reach 6,000 tons, and 10,000 tons in eight to ten years. Those are big numbers, up from official reserve holdings of 1,054 tons in 2009. By comparison, today the United States holds the largest amount of gold, with about 8,100 tons.

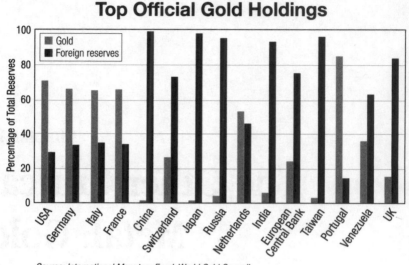

Top Official Gold Holdings

Source: International Monetary Fund, World Gold Council

Interestingly, one of the objections the bank official expressed about gold is that the total market worldwide—about $5 trillion—was too small to play a major role in China's reserves. But gold at twice the price—consistent with massive Chinese accumulation—would no longer be too small. Upon closer inspection there was no contradiction in the two statements.

China wants to increase more than just its government stockpile of gold. It is also encouraging its citizens to buy gold. An increasing number of banks have been given licenses to sell the yellow metal. Moreover, Chinese television ads have regularly presented gold as an excellent investment. A Chinese citizen walking into a bank looking to buy gold will be given the red carpet treatment, literally. The salesperson will place various gold weights on a red felt mat, ranging in size from a small fraction of a kilogram up to one or two kilograms. The metal can be easily purchased from and stored in the same bank for safekeeping.

Think Tiffany & Co. and you get some idea of how the typical Chinese citizen is treated when buying gold. But don't think Tiffany's when you consider the profit Tiffany makes compared with the profit a Chinese bank makes. For the latter, according to our sources, it is 1 percent or less. You can buy gold in the United States too, from a considerable number of accredited dealers, but your chance of buying it at a smaller discount to its underlying value than the Chinese do is very small, if not nil. And it is much easier to find an honest bank in China than an honest dealer in America.

In addition to buying gold on the world market, the Chinese are eager to extract every ounce of the precious metal within their borders. Even though its reserve base of gold yet to be mined is much smaller than those of many other countries—for example, less than half that of South Africa—during the past several years China has been far and away the world's

Gold Production as a Percentage of Reserves

Country	2008 Production*	2009 Production*	Reserves*	Production as % of Reserves
China	285	300	1,900	15.8
Peru	180	180	1,400	12.9
Canada	95	100	1,000	10.0
United States	233	210	3,000	7.0
Papua New Guinea	62	65	1,200	5.4
Ghana	75	85	1,600	5.3
Uzbekistan	85	85	1,700	5.0
Other Countries	446	460	10,000	4.6
Mexico	50	55	1,400	3.9
Australia	215	220	5,800	3.8
Russia	176	185	5,000	3.7
South Africa	213	210	6,000	3.5
Indonesia	60	100	3,000	3.3
Brazil	50	50	2,000	2.5
Chile	39	40	2,000	2.0
World Total (Rounded)	2,260	2,350	47,000	5.0

* In Tons
Source: U.S. Geological Survey

largest producer of the precious metal. During 2010 the Chinese mined more than 15 percent of their gold reserves. Historically, a large percentage of any mineral mined in a year would be about 10 percent of reserves; a percentage as high as 15 percent is nearly unheard of.

The country's desire for gold has been so intense that mining accidents are on the rise. Things have gotten so bad that Zijin Mining, the nation's largest gold miner, has been forced to stop mining on several of its properties. There have also been several reports of fatalities in other gold mining accidents. And the country's reported accidents are very likely just the tip of the iceberg. It is just not possible to mine such a massive portion of reserves without incurring ever more frequent mishaps.

As we discussed in chapter 2, China is desperate for every piece of electronic scrap—and gold is part of some of that scrap, and is just a small reason why the amount of gold the Chinese have cannot even be inferred. But gold from scrap is small potatoes to what the Chinese government and its citizenry have accumulated.

All-Weather Asset

From our perspective, it's clear the Chinese are more determined to accumulate vast reserves of gold than perhaps any other country. Look at their desperate mining rates, the government's unmatched determination to get their citizens to buy gold, and their reaching out to the World Gold Council (the leading gold miners' trade association) to develop gold-related products as all being solid evidence that the Chinese are more determined to accumulate gold than any other country.

There are a couple of compelling and intertwined reasons for this. The most straightforward is that gold is cheap. Yes, even despite its huge run in recent years, gold is still cheap. Consider the following.

Since the beginning of the twenty-first century very few investments have proved profitable. The exceptions were stocks in emerging countries like China and India, commodities, and shares in countries that were net commodity exporters such as Canada and Australia. But these all took a backseat to gold, which outperformed virtually everything.

Gold prices have risen each year since 2001. From its low of around $250 an ounce in the late 1990s, gold today costs roughly five times more, and its annualized rate of return since 2001 averaged 17 percent—far in excess of the inflation rate and far above returns on almost every other investment. No other major asset class has been so rewarding during this period.

Additionally, the past decade or so is not a one-off phenomenon; gold has withstood the test of time in the five-millennia history in which it has been prized for its beauty and durability. Just consider how it has done in our lifetimes: Since it started trading publicly in the United States in the early 1970s, gold's returns have closely matched those of the S&P 500. Indeed, as of this writing gold and the S&P 500 (including dividends) have almost the same returns over the past two generations!

Traditionally, investors have regarded gold as an inflation hedge. It certainly served that role in the 1970s. However, gold is more than just an inflation hedge or a tool for diversification. It's also a powerful deflation hedge. For example, one way to get an idea of how gold has fared over the long term is to look at the history of Homestake Mining. This gold company, which is now part of Newmont Mining, began trading in 1879 and was listed on the exchange for more years than any other stock. During the deflationary period of the Great Depression, from 1929 to 1936 (when stocks overall lost considerable ground), Homestake's share price went from $65 to $544. Gold also rose 100 percent during the deflationary period from 1814 to 1830. The metal's gains since the beginning of this century were likewise made under deflationary conditions in the developed countries.

In fact, if we look a little deeper, we can see that gold is not really an inflation hedge but a hedge against the debasement of currencies, particularly the U.S. dollar. Gold—especially during times when there are doubts about paper currencies—functions as a currency more than a commodity.

It was used as money for most of history, and it is still the money of last resort when all others fail. More on that later.

Both inflation and deflation can lead to the debasement of currencies, and that's why gold prices rise during both phenomena. Gold prices soared in the 1970s as skyrocketing oil prices along with surging prices for other commodities led to a higher cost of living and thus a weaker dollar. Today, governments around the world are trying to combat deflation (which, as we argued in our preface, is ironically caused by rising commodity prices) and recession by debasing their currencies through massive injections of liquidity and spending. So again, weaker currencies mean higher gold prices. Whatever 'flation we get, it's good for gold.

Still, with gold prices rising so strongly, many have started to wonder if gold is in a bubble—and they question just how high prices can go before they peak. But just because something rises a lot doesn't mean it is at a peak. If the factors propelling it higher are growing stronger and the price of the asset relative to those factors is cheap, the asset could be a better buy at higher prices than at lower ones. Seth Glickenhaus, now in his late nineties, is a Wall Street legend. One of his comments that has remained with us is that purchasing a bankrupt company on a bet that it would survive makes little sense. On the other hand, buying the same company after it had survived bankruptcy and is on its way to prosperity makes complete sense. And so it is with any asset: You don't buy or sell because of where the asset has been but rather because of the factors that are driving it forward. In other words, buying high can sometimes be much more rational than buying low.

With these thoughts in mind there is a ready argument—especially if you believe as we do and the Chinese have averred, that the dollar will continue to be debased—for why the upside for gold is tremendous.

One way to judge whether gold is over- or underpriced is to look at the ratio between the gold supply and the money supply. Compare the ratio of gold, the ultimate hard currency, with the value of paper currencies. However, nations today have very different ways of measuring their respective money supplies. For instance, the United States no longer calculates M3, a broad definition of the nation's money supply, which was a very useful measure in the past.

Another way to evaluate gold is to look at the ratio between gold prices and the nominal gross world product (GWP is like GDP, but for the entire planet), that is, without inflation being factored out. This tells us how much gold there is in the world versus the nominal value of goods produced. Because gold is one commodity that is not consumed or destroyed the same way as say, oil or iron, its price is a good reflection of the total value of its supply.

The simple premise here is that the more volatile and iffy the world's economy is, the greater the need for a shelter, and therefore the larger the ratio of gold should be to underlying economic activity.

Since the early 1970s, the ratio of gold to GWP has averaged 0.65. Today it stands at 0.57, which tells us that gold, relative to our metric, is actually cheap, despite its gains since the beginning of the century. So how high would gold prices need to go before it could be considered overvalued? The last time gold peaked was in 1980, when the ratio averaged 1.72. At the absolute peak in February that year, the ratio was

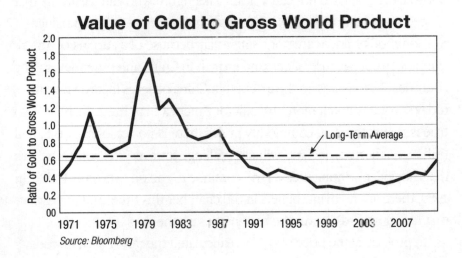

Value of Gold to Gross World Product

Source: Bloomberg

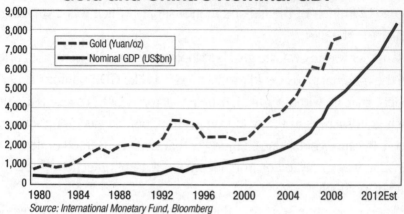

Gold and China's Nominal GDP

Source: International Monetary Fund, Bloomberg

over 2. Consequently, gold prices would have to nearly triple from today's price of around $1,500 an ounce before gold would be considered over-priced relative to its past peak. Specifically, we would be looking at a gold price of $4,300 per ounce.

However, from the Chinese perspective, gold's potential could even be higher. In the 1980s, for instance, there were ready answers as to what was wrong with the world and how it could be fixed. Today, the solutions are not so clear. We have no Paul Volcker–like figure who can assure us that by stepping on the monetary brakes commodity prices will stop rising.

Commodity prices are not rising today because of a surplus of American money but because of demand growth in China and other developing countries. That means, to the extent that China believes in its own growth, today's world is much more difficult for America than it was in 1980. Also true is that with rising commodity prices there is no reason that U.S. real (inflation-adjusted) income will stop falling, yet every reason to believe that the dollar printing presses will continue to run on overtime. Unlike in 1980, there are no magic bullets in the chamber this time, and the cavalry isn't racing toward us over the horizon to save the day.

In projecting the price of gold we calculated the ratio based on today's

GWP. Over the next five years, if you assume world growth will rise some 5 percent annually (remember, this is nominal growth, not real growth, so that's a safe assumption), then the price gold must reach to return the ratio to its previous peak will also rise. Doing the math results in a five-year target for gold prices of about $5,500 per ounce.

Returning to what we said above, even this high target assumes that the process of currency debasement will be no worse than it was in the 1970s. In fact, it could be much worse, which would mean the gold-to-GWP ratio could rise considerably higher before peaking. And, indeed, from the Chinese perspective a worse scenario for America and the developed world would be correlated with continued strong growth in their economy and other developing economies. Going a step further, even if the Chinese thought their growth was going to fall by the wayside, they would still want gold in anticipation of the massive worldwide deflation that would follow. The bottom line is that until we have a basis for low-inflationary economic growth—meaning growth without currency debasement—as we had in the 1990s, gold prices will continue to rise in an accelerating trend. Or at least that is very likely what the Chinese believe.

Medium of Exchange

Other than just believing that gold is cheap, the Chinese probably have something else in mind as well. Let's suppose you are a country with a great deal of copper reserves and you want to sell some copper in exchange for a currency that will allow you to buy other assets. One country offers you a certain amount of gold, which, because there is just a fixed amount of the precious metal in the world, represents a fixed percent of the world's 165,000 tons or so of gold. Another country offers you paper currency whose current value is equivalent to the amount of gold the other country has offered. Which would you take?

If you knew the currency could immediately be exchanged for assets that would rise in value relative to the price of gold, it would be a no-brainer, you'd take the currency. Indeed, that was the situation in the 1990s when the economy and the market were rapidly appreciating and money supply growth, which averaged about 4 percent a year, was a lot less than GDP growth and dramatically less than the annual gains in the stock market.

But that was the 1990s. In today's world we are printing dollars hand over fist, growth in the economy is much less than the growth in the number of dollars printed, median incomes are declining, and gains in many financial assets are nil. If you exchange your copper (or oil or any other hard asset) for dollars you will be getting in exchange an ever smaller share of a currency that is readily convertible into other assets that are not going up. With gold, the worst that can happen is that you get a constant share of a currency that can be exchanged for any asset you want. Look at it like this: If the number of dollars is increasing then the seller of copper is going to want more and more of them for his copper, which is in finite supply. That is not true for gold, whose supply is also fixed.

If you are in the unfortunate position of holding a lot of dollars (or any other currency that's in the same boat) and in need of a lot of commodities, both now and in the future, you really don't have many choices. You have to buy the commodities that you need for whatever price you have to pay—and to make sure you can buy more in the future—you will have to buy gold. And what goes for America would, of course, go for any country that is forced to print more and more currency to stay afloat.

The winners in this endgame are commodities and gold. If demand for commodities temporarily drops, then gold—even though it will be in less demand—will outperform. But when demand for commodities is rising, then commodities are likely to outperform a strong-performing gold market.

In a world in which scarce commodities have a dramatic and negative effect on the economies of the developed countries—which is precisely what the United States has experienced so far throughout the twenty-first century—the countries that control commodities and gold are in the cat-bird's seat. Their goods can easily be exchanged for whatever else they need.

Keep in mind that there is a distinction between commodities and gold. Eventually commodities are going to be in such short supply that whoever owns them will want to hang on to what they have. As we discussed in chapter 7, we are already seeing signs of this resource nationalism in many countries—in China with rare earths, and in Saudi Arabia, where in 2010 King Abdullah said that he wanted to halt oil exploration in order to save remaining oil reserves for future Saudi generations. Laws and taxes, such as those passed by India during mid-2010 to restrict the exporting of iron ore, are likely to become commonplace as the scarcity of commodities increases.

Ironically, the advantage of gold is that it has very few industrial uses and whatever uses there are can be substituted. However, the value of gold is going to stay around—which is one reason it is the ideal currency in troubled times. This also means the country that controls gold can control its fate to the extent that any country can do so. For China, the bigger its position in gold, the more likely it will be to acquire the resources it needs to develop. Equally important, the more gold its citizens own, the greater the control the government has over its citizens' wealth and well-being.

Also true is that a massive hoard of gold makes it possible to back up your paper currency with gold. So the Chinese would be able to say that you can exchange a yuan for a certain amount of gold (which, of course, would be less than the current value of the yuan). And this, in turn, would make the yuan itself a close substitute for gold. In a world of resource scarcity, controlling gold is as close as you come to controlling your fate.

Americans, meanwhile, continue to largely view gold not as an asset, but as just a pretty metal to be fashioned into jewelry. Ask most brokers, financial advisors, or investors, for that matter, to name the most important asset classes these days and chances are you'll get the pat response of stocks, bonds, and cash. Commodities, and gold in particular, if they are named at all, will be relegated to a small 5 or at most 10 percent weighting in a portfolio. Yet in today's world of an ever-shrinking greenback, miniscule bond yields, and rising resource costs, gold is far and away the most important asset class investors—or a country—can own.

Chapter 12

China's Additional Strengths

We've established that China is getting an excellent head start on the United States in its preparations for the emerging era of resource scarcity, a period that is destined to fuel a serious rivalry between our two nations. It's a rivalry that someday could lead to open conflict.

Each day we delay in getting serious about constructing an alternative energy network puts the Chinese that much further ahead of us in what is akin to an arms race that we cannot afford to lose. Hesitation will only add to the cost going forward as competition heats up for everything from the iron ore used in the steel to manufacture wind pylons to the copper needed for a smart grid to the rare earth elements essential to make efficient electric motors.

China's early mover status installing wind farms and solar power arrays isn't the only advantage they have. Despite being much poorer than the United States in the aggregate, the Middle Kingdom enters this era in far better shape financially, with numerous tools at its disposal to draw upon if needed that will make the development of alternative energies far less costly than it will be for the United States. In the interim, our coffers are increasingly barren, which will weaken our resolve to act.

In many respects China is essentially starting from scratch. Rather than having to replace existing parts of its power delivery system, the country is quite often laying new lines for its smart grid that didn't exist previously. This is being carried out under orders from the central government, with minimal red tape to add to the expense or time required to complete the job. This is a job that was going to be done anyway, but just as they essentially leapfrogged with the introduction of wireless phone systems rather than stringing costly first-generation fixed lines, they'll largely incur this major expense only once, not twice.

The United States, in contrast, has already sunk considerable sums into its existing power grid, which is controlled by a diverse amalgamation of electric utilities, each answerable to state regulators who determine the rates the utilities can charge customers to recover the installation cost. Both the utilities themselves and the state regulators may balk at the added expense of replacing the existing power grid, even if the new one is better capable of handling the demands of getting electricity from variable power sources (solar when the sun is shining, wind when it's blowing) to where it's needed, when it's needed. This involves not only just delivering the juice, but also monitoring its customers' usage to anticipate demand.

Even if the utilities are eager to embrace greater alternative power generation capabilities, they are likely to face strong opposition from regulators looking to shield their financially strapped citizens from having to pay higher monthly electricity bills. This could hinder the speed with which the United States adopts alternative energy, even as rising prices for coal and natural gas make those alternative power sources more cost-competitive. But this is really the least of our worries.

The necessary U.S. crash program to bring about a full-fledged alternative energy system is too big to leave entirely to the free market. Utilities alone will not get the job done; it will require the considerable resources of the federal government as well if we are to pay the estimated $25 trillion-plus price tag of an alternative energy power system and get it built in a timely fashion.

But the United States is quickly becoming a beggar nation, ill-equipped to cover the bill. The country is straddled with a national debt that exceeds $14 trillion and is rapidly rising. The government's budget deficit for fiscal 2010 came in at more than $1.3 trillion on the heels of a $1.42 trillion deficit in 2009. In addition, future deficits are currently projected to total $9.1 trillion in the coming decade. Merely servicing the national debt is becoming increasingly more daunting.

This state of affairs prompted Admiral Michael Mullen, chairman of the Joint Chiefs of Staff, in August 2010 to call our debt "the most significant threat to our national security." The amount spent servicing the debt is now approaching the size of the Defense Department's annual budget. As the level of outstanding debt rises, it leaves fewer funds available for discretionary spending, including for national defense. It also stands to postpone the day by which this country gets serious about moving to alternative energy production, which, as we've made the case, will only rise with time. And the debt time-bomb situation is likely to get worse. That's because if it is to entice investors, the U.S. Treasury will have to offer ever higher rates of interest on its bonds, substantially adding to the cost of financing our debt.

A soaring debt load is what led so many European countries into trouble in 2010. Excessive spending was also behind the debt repudiation in Mexico, Argentina, Russia, and many other countries in recent decades. And it's the reason why the United States' AAA sovereign credit rating is now in question. Yet our federal debt being close to exceeding our GDP doesn't even tell the whole story. Excluded from that figure are the unfunded liabilities of the Social Security system, for instance. We are going to need deep cuts in entitlements to help get our financial house in order. But special interests, with the ear of every U.S. senator and congressional representative on Capitol Hill, will strongly fight those cuts.

With short-term interest rates having been cut to zero to combat the deflationary effects of the financial crisis and the anemic economy, and with no other arrows left in its quiver, the Federal Reserve has been reduced to monetizing the debt (essentially printing money to buy newly issued Treasury bonds). Together, our colossal debt load, zero interest rate policy, and the Fed's quantitative easing will keep the U.S. dollar under pressure, ultimately raising our cost for raw materials considerably. In the long run, the effects from all this stand to make the painful inflation of the 1970s seem like a walk in the park.

So far, the dollar's descent has been slowed because as the world's reigning reserve currency, it is widely seen as the best house in a bad neighborhood. At a certain point, however, the tenants are going to move out in favor of nicer digs elsewhere. Neither the euro nor the yen are up to the task of replacing the buck, though. The euro, in fact, may not even be long for this world, judging by the turmoil in the EU in recent years and the structural imbalances that brought about that instability.

China's capital markets aren't sufficiently developed for the renminbi, or yuan as it's also known, to assume the role of reserve currency—yet. But this will change, and perhaps change quickly.

Regardless of what replaces the greenback as the world's reserve currency, be it a single currency or a basket in the form of Special Drawing Rights from the International Monetary Fund (which China publicly favors but has not pressed the issue), once we lose that "safe haven" status the outcome will harm our country. And China's leaders are very much aware of this.

They've Got Us Pegged

In contrast to the United States, China's financial position, plus factors at work with its economy, put the Chinese in the driver's seat. In the last chapter we discussed China's love affair with gold and its realization of the metal's importance as a medium of exchange in a world in which vital resources are increasingly scarce. Here we want to touch on some of the other advantages China has going for it for the difficult times that lie ahead.

To maintain a competitive edge for its exports, China has long pegged its yuan to the U.S. dollar. As a result, the yuan is widely viewed as being drastically undervalued. For years the currency was pegged at the fixed rate of 8.28 yuan to the dollar. As China became the world's leading manufacturing center, it ran huge trade surpluses with many industrialized countries, especially the United States. This has led to a growing chorus calling for Beijing to revalue.

But despite repeated appeals from its trading partners to allow the yuan to float freely, the government has remained steadfast in maintaining that any changes in its exchange rate policy will be based on its assessment of its own interests, not on external pressure. It has, however, paid lip service to outside calls for a stronger yuan. In 2005 the Chinese instituted a floating peg, where the yuan is managed using a basket of currencies. In the period since then, the currency has appreciated quite a bit, and as of this writing stands at 6.5 yuan to the dollar. If it were completely free-floating, it might well appreciate to around 5.

When it suits their needs, most likely only after commodity prices have risen substantially above today's levels, the Chinese will revalue their currency. Doing so will sharply reduce their costs for raw materials. Of course this will raise our tab for the same resources.

U.S. policymakers, both in the White House and on Capitol Hill, are clamoring about the glacial pace with which the Chinese are moving to revalue their currency. They should be careful what they wish for. While such chest-pounding may score points with the voters in their districts, the effects of a stronger yuan would actually be harmful to U.S. consumers, raising prices for many goods, while doing little to actually improve our trade deficit.

One mechanism Congress could use to attempt to force China's hand on this score would be trade restrictions. China exports three times as much to the United States as it imports from us, so it would seem China has a strong incentive to see a free flow of goods between the two countries. But difficult economic times frequently give rise to nationalism. That was certainly the case in 2009, as globally new requests for protection from imports in the first half of the year rose 18.5 percent over the same period in 2008, according to the World Bank–sponsored Global Anti-dumping Database.

So far the spats between the two nations have been minor, such as the United States imposing tariffs on Chinese-made tires and accusing the country of dumping certain steel products. The Chinese government responded with tariffs of their own on U.S. steel imports and threats of tariffs on U.S.-made auto parts and chickens. Growing resentment here of China's currency manipulations, and of its persistent trade surplus, could lead to an escalation in trade barriers, which would no doubt be met in kind. While both China and the United States are mindful of the damage wrought by global trade barriers during the Great Depression, we can't entirely rule out a repeat performance, though the threat seems remote. But the truth is, if it does come to that, China is in far better shape to weather a trade war than the United States.

But rather than deviating from the course they're currently on, or risking rising trade tension, a step the Chinese could take to reduce the size of their trade surplus without resorting to allowing the yuan to appreciate would be to raise workers' pay. Though that would reduce the competitiveness of China's exports, as companies would be forced to raise prices, such a move would boost domestic spending dramatically. For an example of the positive effect this would have, consider Henry Ford's decision to double his workers' wages to a level that would allow them to afford one of the Model Ts they were helping to build on Ford's assembly line. To that end, with hundreds of millions of Chinese consumers eager to buy their first car, China's growth from a doubling in wages would be staggering.

In the meantime, the communist government is slowly making moves to raise the yuan's role in international trade. It has inked currency swap deals with several nations, including Argentina, Indonesia, South Korea, and Singapore. These swaps allow the countries to pay for Chinese imports with yuan rather than U.S. dollars. The government has also allowed select Chinese firms in Shanghai and four cities in Guangdong province to pay for imports with yuan. As with so many other programs introduced in China since the beginning of the reform movement under Deng Xiaoping, this trial is a prelude to what will become the full-scale use of the yuan in international trade.

If the country can make serious headway in shifting its economy from being driven by exports to a more consumer-oriented one (more on that in a moment), there will be less need to shelter export-oriented enterprises from potentially harmful foreign competition. That would give the government the leeway to allow for the full convertibility of China's capital account, which would help solidify the yuan's position as a replacement for the U.S. dollar as the world's reserve currency.

The Chinese also have $3 trillion in foreign currency reserves, notably including more than $1 trillion in U.S. Treasury securities. They can put that to work to buy resources on the open market and, increasingly, to acquire mining operations around the globe to ensure the availability of resources for years to come.

Already they have sharply reduced the average maturity of their U.S. bond holdings. Should a day come when they decide to greatly reduce their holdings in U.S. Treasury bonds altogether, we will have little choice but to buy back this paper to keep our interest rates from rising. So in effect, the United States is likely to inadvertently aid China's purchase of commodities in the future.

But China's real ace in the hole is that it has comparatively little external debt—approximately $330 billion as this book went to press. The government will have absolutely no problem finding willing buyers for more yuan-denominated bonds, given the country's healthy rate of growth and the potential for its currency to strengthen considerably. By using its own sovereign debt (backed by rising tax revenue) to foster domestic consumption rather than relying on foreign capital and a dependence on exports, China can really prosper, regardless of the health of the world's more mature economies.

China's banking system is another instrument the country will draw upon to achieve its lofty ambitions. Its financial markets may be less developed than ours, but Chinese banks have been notably more stable than their Western counterparts in recent years. The largest banks in America raised tens of billions of dollars through public offerings in 2009–10, with the proceeds going to repay government bailout funds and shore up their fragile balance sheets. Several Chinese banks likewise floated huge initial public offerings in 2010. Agriculture Bank of China and Industrial and Commercial Bank of China, for instance, each raised around $22 billion, in what were the largest IPOs on record. But instead of using the funds merely to stay in business as was the case with their American counterparts, the Chinese banks put the capital they raised to productive use in expanding their country's economy. The loans these banks have made today for infrastructure construction, including alternative energy production, will pay off in spades in the years ahead—not just for the banks, but the Chinese economy as a whole.

On the other hand, many American banks remain solvent only by virtue of questionable accounting rule changes and the unspoken promise of another government rescue if needed. Rather than making loans that would better the country, the bankers, who are intent on shrinking their balance sheets, are content to invest in risk-free Treasury paper, all while the banks and their Wall Street advisors are earning billions through the use of high-frequency trading strategies, which give them an unfair advantage over their customers in the equities market and do nothing to boost the country's productivity and, indeed, limit the growth potential of the U.S. economy. Retail customers, knowing that it's not a level playing field, that they're at a disadvantage to Wall Street's powerful computers, are disinclined to provide the risk capital that could be used to put this country on the path to energy independence.

In essence, key participants in the U.S. financial markets are focused on the short term, measured not just quarter to quarter, but in terms of milliseconds. China's financial system, meanwhile, is functioning as it should: Its banks are in fine shape and they are making loans with the big picture in mind, thinking ten to twenty years or longer into the future, providing access to capital that is being used to build alternative energy infrastructure. And thanks to the Chinese government's majority stake in the country's banks, they truly are "too big to fail."

Living in the City

In the thirty years leading up to 2009, China's economic juggernaut was driven by exports of cheap goods manufactured by the country's vast throngs of workers. These individuals toiled for long hours in what by Western standards were horrible conditions for miniscule wages. But when the United States and Europe tipped into recession and the financial crisis was at its worst in late 2008, China felt the impact through no fault of its own. Most lending stopped and letters of credit were no longer available. International trade came to a halt and goods piled up at the ports. The collapse in foreign demand sliced China's record 2008 trade surplus of close to $300 billion by more than a third. The once humming assembly lines of the factories along China's coast were either silenced or at best reduced to producing far less than they had in previous years. The result was that millions of migrant workers suddenly found themselves out of work, forced to return to their towns and villages in China's interior.

One of the painful lessons China's leaders learned from this is that they needed to be more self-reliant rather than depending on the now tapped-out American consumer to fuel growth. Though consumption would resume, it was evident that U.S. consumers would not quickly, if ever, return fully to their spendthrift, credit-driven habits of yesteryear.

To get its factories back up to speed and its tens of millions of unemployed back to work, China's leadership initiated a plan to dramatically realign the economy, placing an emphasis on domestic consumption rather than pinning its hopes on a return of exports. A large part of the country's 4 billion yuan ($585 billion, or, more accurately, $2.5 trillion on a purchasing power parity basis) stimulus package was devoted to building up its infrastructure, including substantial spending on alternative energy. This public spending will help boost the country's long-term growth while leaving it far better positioned to withstand resource scarcity. But another facet of the country's plan was designed to get its citizens, notorious savers, to open their wallets.

Lacking a social safety net comparable to what we're familiar with here in the West, and due to structural differences in their economy (such as large down payments required for home buyers), China's savings rate approaches 40 percent—the highest among the world's major economies. We've already discussed how the government is eager to get its citizens to use some of these savings to purchase gold. It has also actively spurred its people to buy consumer goods, with generous subsidies for appliances and automobiles, for instance. The government is also likely to step up its social spending, a move that will boost the country's long-term productivity and will reduce the need for its people to save so much.

The sheer size of China's populace, an internal market of more than 1.3 billion, gives the country a certain gravitational pull that's impossible to match. And whereas consumers represent about 70 percent of the U.S. economy, they comprise a mere 35 percent of China's economy. As its low per capita personal consumption rises it will fuel considerable growth, alleviating the need to rely on exports.

An even bigger factor that will spur China's growth in the coming years, lessen the importance of global trade for the country's economy, and better position it to take advantage of its alternative energy production is the drive to greater urbanization. The Chinese Academy of Social Sciences, a top government think tank, predicts that China's urbanization rate will climb from 52 percent in 2015 to 65 percent by 2030—at which time it will have at least two hundred cities with populations of a million

China's Rapid Urbanization

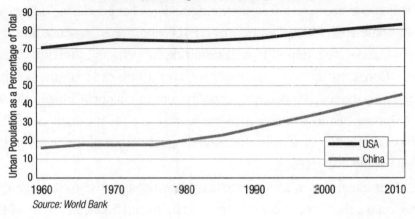

Source: World Bank

or more people. In contrast, the urbanization rate in the U.S. today is approximately 82 percent.

For China, this means some 400 million people will move off the farm and into cities in the next twenty years. This will be carefully planned by the government and orchestrated under the country's hukou laws, which dictate that access to social services, including low-cost health care, schooling, and pensions, is based on residency permits.

A large percentage of these subsistence farmers currently have no electricity or running water in their mud-brick homes. Not only will they be moving to modern urban housing, but they will be furnishing those flats with refrigerators, stoves, air conditioners, flat-panel televisions, and other appliances ubiquitous to today's lifestyles. In addition to housing, roads, sanitation, water and power lines, schools, hospitals, and the like will all have to be built to accommodate this unprecedented mass migration and industrialization, efforts that will sustain China's 10 percent annual expansion well into the future. This growth, along with the resulting productivity gains and rising incomes, will make paying for the country's alternative energy infrastructure that much easier.

Of course, while expanding its internal consumer base will make

China less reliant on exports to the United States and the rest of the West, it will also exacerbate resource shortages. Big-ticket goods, including cars and home appliances, are not only energy-intensive to produce and use, but are resource-intensive as well, requiring copper, steel, and other materials. Consider that just the copper required to make all of this possible can easily exceed 100 pounds per apartment unit alone. China is already consuming nearly 40 percent of the world's copper production, and its growth threatens to absorb the entire annual output of the metal in the next twenty-five years.

This expansion will drive metals prices through the roof. Nevertheless, unlike the United States, China is well situated financially to meet the daunting challenge of rapidly moving to an alternative energy economy.

Chapter 13

Potential Pitfalls: China's Infrastructure, Food, and Water

As we write this, many extremely well-schooled investors, economists, and analysts are convinced that China has passed its peak. Jim Chanos, for example, a legendary short seller, thinks China has overbuilt its infrastructure to the point where the whole country has become a bubble of epic proportions. Ken Rogoff, who coauthored the extremely well-respected *This Time Is Different: Eight Centuries of Financial Folly*, also argues that a financial collapse in China is inevitable. There are also many who think China will falter as it transforms its economy from being led by growth in exports to one led by consumer demand.

We completely disagree with these naysayers. In fact, our sense is that they are doing more harm than good by fostering an attitude of American complacency toward China—an attitude that could bring this nation to its knees, which China has already started to do. But still, we do hope we have missed something fundamental, and our purpose here is to discuss what we may have overlooked in our assessment that China is in the process of eating our lunch. Is China clearly destined to rule a third-rate America?

Of course, there is the possibility that we are wrong for reasons we don't understand—and it is those reasons that might explain the current complacency of the U.S. government. After all, it seems clear that the best minds in Washington do not yet view China as a major strategic threat. Or at least they do not agree that the problem is massive in scope.

America, for instance, tends to see rare earth elements as necessary for defense but not as a critical cog in overall economic and energy security. As for copper and silver, they are not even on America's radar screen as potentially scarce metals. Perhaps government scientists have carefully considered the problem and have seen something we missed. But unfortunately there is no evidence to support this view.

We could also be wrong for a wonderful reason—a major technology breakthrough that might come along. In this case, the world would no longer be zero-sum or lose-win but win-win. What kind of breakthrough would make the difference? In chapter 8 we discussed graphene, an experimental one-atom-thick carbon-based material, as a remote possibility. Another possible savior technology could offer would be a way of accessing massive amounts of very cheap energy. Cold fusion, if it had worked, might have been an example. Cheap fusion could also be a road to a new energy economy. Though most scientists pooh-pooh the idea of cold fusion, there are a number of researchers who continue to pursue this course. Our view is that after more than a generation of trying, there probably are some interesting results, but none that would point to a full-scale rollout of a brand-new miracle technology, capable of the massive scaling that would be needed to segue into a new energy platform.

Perhaps there could be breakthroughs in existing renewable technologies. On this score the energy source with the greatest potential by far would be solar—and it is in these areas that we should try to encourage the most research. Currently wind is far cheaper than solar and much more easily employed, but there is far less room for improvement in terms of resource efficiencies. And because solar is many times more plentiful than wind, it offers much greater potential if technological breakthroughs can be achieved.

As we discussed earlier, we are currently doing little more than paying lip service to solar energy. The Chinese, by contrast, are following the same road with solar that enabled us to so dramatically lower the costs of electronics in the 1960s and 1970s. Even though solar is not being employed yet on a large scale within China, by becoming the world leader in manufacturing solar modules it has provided a path for itself to move dramatically up the learning curve and reduce costs. Remember, it was massive government orders of electronics that got America moving so rapidly up that learning curve. And for the record, our dramatic edge in airplane design also came from massive government purchases of airplane parts. Cost-saving manufacturing would be a major positive, but probably not enough to push solar to a civilization-saving energy source.

A real breakthrough in solar energy could come from two possible sources: huge improvements in energy storage or massive increases in efficiencies. Indeed, it would probably have to be a combination of both. Clearly, one limitation of solar energy is that it's only available during the daytime. If it is to be a critical standalone energy source, there will have to be efficient ways of storing energy generated during the day for nighttime use. So far we have made scant progress in this area.

Arguably the best way of storing energy would be with superconducting cable. In simple terms, electricity generated during the day could be stored in circular superconducting loops. Remember, the advantage to superconductors is that they do not leak electricity. What goes into the loop would stay in the loop, whereas the typical coal-fired power plant today loses about a third of the coal's energy potential in generating electricity, with additional energy lost as that electricity traverses the transmission grid on its way to our homes.

As you might guess, there are a number of problems associated with superconducting storage. Most important is that it costs money—a lot of it—to keep the cables cool. Unfortunately, there has been very little progress in delivering materials that are superconducting at temperatures much above the level of liquid nitrogen, approximately minus 300 degrees Fahrenheit, as opposed to minus 450 before the advent of "high temperature" superconductivity. The second is that the materials that do conduct at the still very low temperature of minus 300 degrees are brittle and therefore difficult and costly to fashion into loops. And finally, superconducting loops also require a great deal of copper, which as you now know is likely to remain in very short supply.

Perhaps there could be a major breakthrough in superconductivity—one in which materials are found that are flexible and superconductive at room temperature. There is nothing in the laws of physics to preclude such a breakthrough. In a world in which science's reliance on combinatorics has trumped intuitive insights, the odds are small—but it is not irrational to hope.

A breakthrough in superconductivity would probably have to be accompanied by a breakthrough in solar efficiencies as well. As solar materials convert more of the sun's light and heat into electricity, less silver and indium would be needed to create solar energy. Here there are basic physical constraints in that as solar cells are heated, they become increasingly less efficient. Stanford researchers may have made a partial breakthrough in this area, figuring out a way to use both the light and heat of the sun to generate electricity. Yet even if this innovation can be scaled, it would still leave us with storage problems.

Although we cannot do precise calculations, it is likely the case that even with major advancements in storage and efficiency, resource constraint continues to play a major role in limiting solar energy. For example, solar collectors that converted both heat and light into electricity would still require the resources used to manufacturer the collectors—and these resources would likely include copper, steel, and silver. Though obviously we can't predict what some new materials might be, it is certainly possible that the same resource constraints would likely apply to novel technologies—very high-temperature superconductivity—as well.

The most likely scenario remains more or less the technology status quo. Advances will likely be predominantly confined to scaled gains in manufacturing, the lion's share of which will accrue to the fastest-growing manufacturers—in other words, the Chinese. In short, this leaves them better positioned than America for what lies ahead.

Of Bubbles and Necessity

The failure of technology to deliver a stunning breakthrough will be potentially catastrophic for the developed world. Still, there is no guarantee that China, despite some gains in manufacturing efficiencies, will come away smiling. In fact, that is very unlikely.

But even more remote, at least in the relatively near term, is that China will falter because of the usual suspects mentioned at the beginning—financial bubbles and the like. Any country that grows as fast as China is going to generate bubbles in at least some assets. Prior to the 2008 meltdown there was a huge bubble in Chinese stocks. In the sixteen months between June 2006 and October 2007, Chinese stocks more than tripled—gains that matched the performance of America's NASDAQ in its most manic phase in the 1998–2000 period. But as we know, China survived that bubble. Yes, their stock market collapsed in the wake of the financial crisis, but the economy (unlike ours in 2000–2002) continued to motor along.

One of the current "bubbles" that has grabbed the attention of so many is in real estate. Without a doubt, certain parts of the real estate market there are overinflated—possibly wildly so. The first thing to note here is that there is an inevitability to inflation in some assets when you have unprecedented government spending and surging growth. But more important is that the worst inflation has been confined to very specific real

estate—the most desirable apartments in the most desirable cities. And as
of early 2011, it seems the government has controlled these excesses with
only modest increases in interest rates.

Ironically, there are more serious problems in Chinese real estate that
have not made headlines. There is a desperate need to build low-cost
housing on a scale the world has never seen before. The year 2009 was a
first—the first time in modern history that the amount of incremental low-
cost housing in China's cities matched the creation of urban families in
those cities. If China is to succeed in its urbanization plans and hence its
plans to transform its economy into one led by the consumer, then 2009's
frantic pace will have to be matched every year for at least a generation or
more.

Incidentally, while some point to labor strikes in China as symp-
tomatic of growing unrest, this is not the case. These strikes in fact are
largely sanctioned (or they would have been outlawed at the start) by the
government as a part of putting greater wages in the hands of consumers. Indeed, there have been reports that the Chinese are even considering capping the salaries of CEOs—especially those of state-controlled
companies.

Then there is gold, which we talked about in a previous chapter. China
has been urging its citizens to accumulate gold and making it very easy
to do so. As gold prices advance, so will the wealth of its citizenry. China's success since the 1970s—a period which it negotiated a number of
transitions—is a strong argument that it will succeed in this transition,
except for the caveat that it will need tremendous amounts of resources,
which even it may not be able to collect (as we discuss below).

Chanos and others have argued that China faces much more than
just a bubble in residential real estate—that the country has vastly overbuilt its infrastructure. To buttress this case they show pictures of empty
cities (newly built cities that have been put together with roads, buildings,
government offices, mass transit systems, and indeed everything but
residents). The pessimists argue that the nature of Chinese economic

management is such that heads of provincial governments are rewarded to the extent that they make certain growth benchmarks.

That is, building a city even if it is not needed and remains empty can still count as economic growth. For example in the September 6, 2010, issue of *Barron's*, Alan Abelson, the brilliant cynic of virtually everything, offered comments from Ben Simpfendorfer, an economist at the Royal Bank of Scotland, who claims China has vastly overbuilt infrastructure. Specifically, the economist was quoted as saying that "in the case of China, there is a risk the country is spending too much on building highways and factories, resulting in overcapacity and bad debts." But we think the Chinese are much smarter than that.

First, if you are intent on urbanizing an extraordinary number of people, it is necessary to have a place for them to move. You would not encourage your son or friend to move into an empty lot any more than the Chinese would want to encourage their rural residents to move into a city that does not exist. Building on the scale of what's taking place in China means some mistakes are going to be made, but the Chinese are more intent on avoiding the serious problems that have plagued so many other emerging nations that have experienced mass migrations to urban centers.

The communist government is all too aware that its continued existence rests on its ability to keep the peasants, its core power base, happy. By having ready-built cities with adequate housing in place before tens of millions of people arrive, the Chinese hope to avoid the poverty, crime, and social instability common in cities across East Asia, Africa, and Latin America. And unlike other countries contending with the same issues, China has the governmental infrastructure in place to successfully carry out its plans.

The second reason is much more realistic but never mentioned. The Chinese—to the extent that we are right—want to build the cities now when resources are relatively plentiful and not that expensive. In as few as five to ten years, building materials are likely to be far more expensive than they are today. Waiting on urbanization while a multitrillion-dollar build-out of alternative energies gets under way would represent an impossible demand on resources.

Countries that are urbanizing require a great deal of infrastructure to precede the actual migration of citizens to the cities—much more than American economists appear to understand. Even with the so-called over-building of infrastructure, newspapers both in America and China in 2010 headlined stories of massive traffic jams in the Middle Kingdom, which are the result of transporting goods from one city to another. What this suggests is that, if anything, China has not built enough infrastructure.

Infrastructure is also vital for the building of renewable energies. One of the major issues concerning iron ore is the roads and trains to trans-port the thousands of tons that have to be carried. How would you build windmills or solar panels in western China if there were not roads for transporting the necessary resources? Many historians credit the postwar boom in America to the interstate highway system. China is drawing from our playbook.

Also remember that one purpose of the interstate highway system, which was initiated under Eisenhower, was to improve America's military preparedness. Ready routes for transporting equipment and personnel from one site to another are vital to a strong military. And so it is with China, which has to exert control over more than 1.3 billion people. They know that communication throughout the country is a vital necessity. There is also China's need to protect itself from outside threats, which may become much more real as resource scarcity takes hold.

And this leads us to another problem that China will surely face—competition for resources from other developing countries. In this vein, if we look at China's largest neighbor, Russia, we see a country whose greatest strength and weakness is a true lack of infrastructure. How has this been a strength? Both Napoleon and Hitler were defeated in Russia because of the country's lack of infrastructure, which prevented the invad-ing armies from setting up adequate supply lines.

Today, of course, Russia is not worried about foreign attacks and instead views its lack of infrastructure as a major economic weakness. In Siberia, for example, the country's ability to explore and drill for oil is hampered by the lack of roads and basic transportation. This tells us something about China and why it has been so successful in mining basic materials. For most metals and materials, China mines a larger percentage of its reserves in a year than any other country. A country's infrastructure is strongly related to its ability to search for minerals and therefore vital to its growth. What some analysts see as vanity roads and rail lines are really essential items for its future growth.

A more meaningful question than whether China has too much infrastructure (when in fact it still has massive infrastructure development ahead of it) is what happens when other developing countries get the message that their continued prosperity is dependent on major infrastructure projects. The dreadful fires across western Russia in 2010 certainly brought home this point. A well-chosen quote from Tomas Hirst, writing for the UK's *Prospect* magazine blog on August 9, 2010, is: "To give some idea of the scale, although Russia accounts for over a fifth of the world's landmass it has only half the length of railway lines than in the US with the vast majority running outdated trains that average 25mph. Its road network is also in a dire condition as not only is it one tenth the size of the US's but of that only around 5 per cent is considered 'good quality'.... What the fires have shown is the dire need for this modernisation of infrastructure and the folly of cutting an area that is a necessary condition of further sustained economic growth." By cutting, the author was referring to cuts in the Russian infrastructure budget.

Clearly these comments, which would certainly be echoed by every Muscovite, can be taken as another example of Chinese foresight. Accidents and environmental catastrophes are frequent in China, but they are never as devastating as was the case in Russia. But at the same time these comments are also a major threat to the Chinese. For what happens when Russia and other developing countries finally figure it out—that they will also need massive infrastructure to continue their growth?

The picture on the August 21, 2010, cover of the *Economist* is of the arms of two arm wrestlers. One has a Chinese dragon tattooed on his bicep, the other an Indian tiger. The title of the story is "Contest of the Century." The article points out that since the early 1990s, when per capita income was approximately the same in both countries, China has opened up a huge lead over India. And that is because of China's unbridled emphasis on infrastructure. Now, according to the magazine, India is ready to play catch-up and indeed predicts that over the next five or ten years India's growth could even surpass China's.

But that is not going to happen unless India also focuses almost maniacally on infrastructure development itself. Where will the resources come from, not just for the development of infrastructure but for what comes next, the massive build-out of renewable energies? The point is that the competition for resources is no longer just between America and other developed countries and China, but will exist among a vast array of countries in the developed and developing world.

In early 2009, CIBC World Markets, a respected investment bank, forecast that global infrastructure spending would reach $35 trillion over the next twenty years. It is critical to emphasize that these estimates include very little for what should be the greatest infrastructure project of all: the segue to renewable energies. In the United States, the world's largest economy, only $150 billion is allocated to clean energy. Most of the money the world is expected to spend is earmarked for repairing roads, bridges, and airports, building new hospitals, and digital technologies. Moreover, these estimates allocate only a very small portion to Russia and other developing nations, including China.

Still, the critical point is not so much what the needed expenditures are—they are surely multiples of the $35 trillion—but rather that they are very large and that the projects will certainly consume copious amounts of resources. China is hardly blind to the needs of other countries, and this must be a major reason for its near-desperate search for literally every scrap of important minerals and metals it can find. And it certainly explains its farsighted and maniacal foray into Africa. But in the end—and this is what could trip China up—they may run short and not have enough resources to accomplish their ambitious but necessary economic goals. They could easily end up in the same boat we all will be in—facing a dramatic shortage of resources.

Avi Tiomkin, a highly successful investor and friend, has been more correct on macro trends than anyone else we know. He is convinced that China will be defeated by or implode because of internal strife, led by a rebellious populace. We mention Avi not just because of his acumen but because we think his scenario is the most likely reason why China will fail in its aspirations.

However, the rebellion, if it occurs, will require a catalyst. It will not happen simply because a restive workforce organizes and demands ever greater power and money, as we saw in early 2011 with the revolutions in Tunisia and Egypt and elsewhere in the Arab world.

Protests are not unheard of in China. In 2010, at least 180,000 demonstrations or strikes took place across the country. These protests, however, were often directed at corrupt local officials or foreign factory owners rather than the central government. They were tolerated by Beijing and often had the government's tacit support. But the communists do not abide potentially destabilizing social movements and have proven to be quite adept in their efforts to suppress dissent. Furthermore, and every bit as important, the majority of Chinese believe they have too much to lose from a significant change in the status quo. Unlike the protestors in the Arab world, China's population is well fed, enjoys a rising standard of living, and they see room for unlimited advancement under the current regime. The economic dislocations that would result from a revolution would put their prosperity at risk.

No, the most likely catalyst for widespread revolt in the country will be that the Chinese themselves, despite their massive head start, will face the same problems the rest of the world faces—namely a massive shortage of the essentials of life, everything from energy to food. All the gold in the world cannot buy food if there is no food to be had. If China reaches this situation, the world will face any combination of resource wars and internal chaos. Still, even in the direst of circumstances, the Chinese may still have many advantages.

The most important is that though they have come a long way in a short period of time, they still have far less to fall. Their adjustment to resource shortages will be easier with income per head at $6,500 compared to more than $46,000 in the United States.

H_2 Woes

Also on the short list for most China observers of what could go wrong to derail the country's efforts would be water. China has a lot of water, but some argue not nearly enough to satisfy the needs of a population that will likely approach or exceed 1.5 billion. China currently has the sixth largest water supply in the world, but given the size of its population the country ranks in the bottom quarter in freshwater per capita.

Related to water is agriculture. China has about 7 percent of the world's arable land, from which it must feed nearly a quarter of the world's population. According to Cheng Hefa, Hu Yuanan, and Zhao Jianfu, writing in the respected and peer-reviewed *Environmental Science and Technology* journal in a 2009 article titled "Meeting China's Water Shortage Crisis: Current Practices and Challenges," by 2030 when the country's population is expected to plateau it will be within 5 percent of what is considered the water stress threshold.

Anecdotally, a friend who has spent many years doing business in China and has great respect for their long-term planning and skills has emphasized that the problem is not so much water but *the distribution of water*. The south of the country has plenty of water, whereas the north, home to major cities such as Beijing and Shanghai, has chronic shortages. The same friend believes that water is the most likely critical vulnerability in our China analysis.

We have no argument in that we view water as a major hurdle that China must overcome. But upon analysis, not only do we believe that the Chinese will successfully face up to their water challenge but we believe that their view of water strongly supports our major thesis: While China may believe in resource conservation for the sake of economic security, that policy has little or no stake in climate change. Indeed, a careful reading of the latest literature—especially on the critical challenge of water— suggests that China may actually be comfortable with climate change.

Despite warming temperatures in China, grain yields have increased dramatically over the past forty years. Rice yields have risen by over 50 percent per hectare, corn by more than 100 percent, and wheat by a stunning 300 percent. Warming temperatures, at least so far, have not been unfriendly to China's efforts to increase food supplies. What about the future?

The disparities between the north and south have been a fixture of Chinese geophysics for centuries. So it should not be surprising that China has been planning a solution for about half a century. In 1952 Mao proposed a project that would divert massive amounts of water from the south to the north. Within the last several years Mao's proposal has informed a massive engineering project that will link China's four largest rivers—the Yangtze, Yellow, Huaihe, and Haihe—along three routes that will divert nearly 45 billion cubic meters of water per year from the south to the large urban areas in the north. According to the website Water-Technology.net the estimated cost of the project will be about $62 billion. The first of the three canals, which runs through the North China Plain, is slated for full operation by 2014, although the estimated completion date for the entire project will be around midcentury.

But even if this massive engineering project—the largest ever undertaken—is successful, it will not affect the overall amount of water to which the country has access. If climate change proves to be not only a real phenomenon but one that dramatically influences either the amount or distribution of Chinese precipitation, then the whole engineering project could be for naught.

As of this writing the most definitive study on the effects of putative climate change on Chinese water and agriculture appeared in the journal *Nature*. Entitled "The Impacts of Climate Change on Water Resources and Agriculture in China," the article was authored by sixteen researchers, of whom fifteen were associated with Chinese research centers. The paper's major finding is stated in the abstract:

> We find, however, that notwithstanding the clear warming that has occurred in China in recent decades, current understanding does not allow a clear assessment of the impact of anthropogenic climate change on China's water resources and agriculture and therefore China's ability to feed its people.

The authors note that though China has been warming since 1960, overall precipitation has been more or less constant. There have been some changes in the distribution of precipitation, which on balance suggest that climate change could actually be beneficial to China. In particular, water-starved northern China has been receiving somewhat less rain, while the water-rich south has been receiving more. What do the climate models say about the future? "In northern China, where a decrease in precipitation is observed today, the models surprisingly predict an increase in summer precipitation." The models also predict "a decrease of drought in northeast China." Northeast China is, again, where the major population centers are located.

Glacier melt will be a major factor in Chinese water supply and distribution. Melting glaciers affect river runoff, especially in the very dry western part of the country. The *Nature* article notes, "In the short term [global warming] would be beneficial for irrigated agriculture in arid western China. . . . But in the long term, if a large fraction of the glaciers melt, water shortage may return and become the norm." Yet if we just look at current trends apart from the glaciers we find that over the past decade and more, "surprisingly, arid regions of northwestern China have enjoyed less-severe droughts, as indicated by rising lake levels and increased vegetation cover on the desert margin." In other words, while the fate of the glaciers may be uncertain, current trends favor alleviation of the most severe droughts in the country.

The March 3, 2009, *New York Times Magazine* ran a cover story about the polymath Freeman Dyson, whose negative views on climate change attracted massive criticism. We are not going to comment on the entire article or take a side. But there is one point of Dyson's that struck us— namely, that increased amounts of carbon dioxide could actually increase the world's food supply. That's because carbon dioxide is essential food for plants. And indeed, there are a number of studies that show plants can grow up to 50 percent faster when the concentrations of carbon dioxide are more than double current levels. There are studies that say you cannot consider carbon dioxide by itself; other factors could interfere with the positive effects on plant growth.

Still, no matter how you slice it, increased plant growth has gone hand in hand with higher levels of carbon dioxide. Of course, it could be the case that China's impressive rise in food production is entirely due to better technology. But in short, there is no evidence whatsoever that global warming has interfered with increased food production.

Now put yourself in the position of the Chinese. If your worst fear is an inability to feed your population, you have no reason to fear climate change. This is not to say that climate change will not produce some horrendous effects, but at least on the issue you worry most about, the scientific climatic evidence, if anything, is tilted in favor of your fostering it.

Chapter 14

A Message for America from Confucius

Early on in this book we pointed out how President George W. Bush missed an important opportunity to refocus America's energy policy in the wake of 9/11. So too did Barack Obama following the tragic BP oil spill in the Gulf of Mexico. Their responses to those events bring to mind a quote from the Chinese philosopher Confucius: "A man who has committed a mistake and doesn't correct it is committing another mistake."

Our country is now spending more than $500 billion a year on oil imports alone. That price tag is going rise dramatically in the next few years, as it will for all the other important resources we rely on to run our society. Worse still, those resources may soon not be available at any price. We cannot afford to sit on our hands any longer, doing little to prepare for that calamitous day. Our collective business-as-usual mentality in the face of mounting evidence that resource scarcity is a very real threat stands to be our undoing.

This vulnerability of American society is perhaps best summed up not by an academic, but by the novelist Jonathan Franzen. The author of *Free-dom*, which is considered by many to be the best American novel of its time, Franzen has been compared by some to Tolstoy. "The personality susceptible to the dream of limitless freedom is a personality also prone, should the dream ever sour, to misanthropy and rage." Let's hope Franzen's words remain a warning and not a prophecy fulfilled.

China's culture, it would seem, is better suited for the difficult travails that lie head. Consider this observation from the author of *When China Rules the World*, Martin Jacques: "One of the most fundamental features of Chinese politics concerns the overriding emphasis placed on the country's unity. . . . Its origins lie not in the short period since China became a nation-state, but in the experience and idea of Chinese civilization."

Jacques isn't alone in this view. Princeton astrophysicist J. Richard Gott has sagely observed that the longer an item, institution, civilization, or other entity has existed, everything else being equal, the longer its life expectancy starting from the present. Gott's argument is especially ironic now, in that it was made in 1993 probably as a warning that we should view the fall of Eastern European communism more as a cautionary event than a celebratory one. With thousands of years of tradition behind it, China's culture (with the Communist Party playing the role of modern-day emperor) is more suited for rising to the challenge that lies ahead than America's democracy (and its political infighting), which dates only to the late eighteenth century.

The Potential for Conflict

The Chinese government's rapid rollout of alternative energy leaves no doubt that they are planning for a world where supplies of hydrocarbons and other important minerals are constrained. These are active steps that will help to assure the continuity of their society. If their actions have the effect of combating climate change, so much the better, but everything we've discussed in these pages points to surviving in a resource-depleted world as being far and away their primary objective.

China's foreign policy all the while is shaped by a maxim, "Hide your ambitions and disguise your claws," laid down decades ago by Deng Xiaoping. That is certainly what the People's Republic is doing today with its energy policy, using climate change negotiation talks as a means not only to hide its ambitions to acquire key resources before they become critically scarce but to stall the West's pursuit of that same goal.

Concentrating on its economic development, China is not yet widely seen as a military threat. But as it gets the jump on America in developing its alternative energy infrastructure, it will be in a much better position to project its power, even as our ability to do so is stunted. This power shift will occur simultaneously with our increasing need to protect our supply lines of indispensable resources.

While politicians in the United States still aren't publicly speaking about the world we are heading into, the U.S. military and the armed forces of our allies are studying certain aspects of the subject. A February 2010 study from the U.S. Joint Forces Command that looked at future trends and their implications for national security, for instance, had this to say about energy:

To generate the energy required worldwide by the 2030s would require us to find an additional 1.4 million barrels per day (MBD) every year until then.

During the next twenty-five years, coal, oil, and natural gas will remain indispensable to meet energy requirements. The discovery rate for new petroleum and gas fields over the past two decades (with the possible exception of Brazil) provides little reason for optimism that future efforts will find major new fields.

At present, investment in oil production is only beginning to pick up, with the result that production could reach a prolonged plateau. By 2030, the world will require production of 118 MBD, but energy producers may only be producing 100 MBD unless there are major changes in current investment and drilling capacity.

By 2012, surplus oil production capacity could entirely disappear, and as early as 2015, the shortfall in output could reach nearly 10 MBD.

Energy production and distribution infrastructure must see significant new investment if energy demand is to be satisfied at a cost compatible with economic growth and prosperity. Efficient hybrid, electric, and flex-fuel vehicles will likely dominate light-duty vehicle sales by 2035 and much of the growth in gasoline demand may be met through increases in biofuels production. Renewed interest in nuclear power and green energy sources such as solar power, wind, or geothermal may blunt rising prices for fossil fuels should business interest become actual investment. However, capital costs in some power-generation and distribution sectors are also rising, reflecting global demand for alternative energy sources and hindering their ability to compete effectively with relatively cheap fossil fuels. Fossil fuels will very likely remain the predominant energy source going forward.

Had the study taken the likelihood of the scarcity of other important resources into account, its findings would no doubt be far more severe. And even as it stands, the Joint Forces Command's assessment is almost certainly too optimistic.

In September 2010, the German magazine *Der Spiegel* obtained a leaked document from the Germany Defense Ministry that considered the same issue and reached even more alarming conclusions. Drafted by the Bundeswehr Transformation Center, the report concluded that we have arrived at the point of peak oil. The study sees the impact of peak oil being felt in every aspect of our lives. In addition to supply bottlenecks in manufacturing and agriculture, the study envisions the prospect of a complete failure of markets along with shifting political alliances, political instability, and the threat to the survival of democracy. Among other things, the report implies that there will be resource wars beginning sometime in the next fifteen to thirty years.

Unfortunately, we can't quarrel with these conclusions, and we suspect the Chinese government concurs.

The Costs and Benefits of Preparedness

We estimate the world's total cost for tackling the renewable energy problem to be far greater than the $120 trillion that would be the case if resources were much more plentiful. The cost, therefore, will be many times that of gross world product, and it will still require technological insights and developments not yet imagined. That is a tall order indeed and may prove impossible to achieve. Still, the longer we put off rising to this challenge, the greater the cost—and the greater the likelihood that we will fail in this endeavor.

Of course, many Americans will balk at undertaking such a massive project in light of the debt and deficit problems our country currently faces. Conservatives uniformly agree that the government's top priorities must be to reduce debt and cap, if not lower, taxes—especially for the wealthy, who should be rewarded for innovations that support GDP expansion. Naturally, the only way to achieve both these goals at the same time would be to slash government spending.

Left-wing intellectuals and economists have their own compelling prescription for today's difficult economic climate. According to their version, today's high unemployment is a serious drag on economic growth as well as a social evil. To them, raising taxes on the wealthy would be an acceptable way to balance the budget, reduce government deficits, and take some of the burden off the poor and middle classes. They believe such a policy would also help reduce the extreme gap between rich and poor, which the left sees as another obstacle to growth and stability, as well as an impediment to democracy. The left-wing interpretation regards government spending as a useful tool to prevent excessive hardship until the country gets back on its feet. But again, with deficits so high, the consensus view from the left is that any spending should be only temporary and that the deficit must soon be tackled.

We prefer not to take sides in political discussions, but we think there's an important point that both sides have missed. It begins with the fact that—and we're not being partisan here—the economic stimulus bill of 2009 has to be the most disappointing piece of legislation we've ever seen.

In the first place, any legislation that so divides the country along political lines is a poor way to solve a crisis that affects almost everyone. What we really needed was a plan that would bring people of different political stripes together.

Second, we believe the one thing that could have brought the nation together was a focus on restoring economic growth. Moreover, real, sustained growth cannot come from consumers buying more cars, bigger houses, flat-panel TV sets, designer clothes, or other trappings of our consumer society. Real growth must come from the creation of new industries and new efficiencies. Such a foundation for growth would benefit everyone—rich and poor alike. It would create jobs, benefit investors, and allow the country to maintain a high quality of life.

A critical distinction should be made between spending and investing. In the short run, spending (of the kind born of the American Recovery and Reinvestment Act of 2009 and various industry bailouts undertaken in recent years) can help alleviate near-term economic malaise, but much of it was spending ill-suited for the world in which we now find ourselves.

Instead of spending billions to bail out, say, auto manufacturers, our money should be used to retool and train an army of workers capable of producing solar panels by the millions. Instead of spending billions on highway projects, our money should be committed to building and electrifying railways. Instead of funneling billions into pet projects earmarked by every politician on Capitol Hill, funds should be used to erect a smart grid and wind towers in every suitable location in the country, as well as for the advancement of other promising alternative energies, such as tidal power.

Many corporations have leveraged successfully by employing money in productive enterprises. So too can the government in conjunction with corporate America. *The United States created such a foundation once*

before in history, toward the end of World War II. Sure, the ratio of gov-
ernment debt as a percentage of GDP is approaching 100 percent, which
is an alarming and perhaps unsustainable level. However, this is not the
first time we've hit these heights.

Debt-to-GDP hit its historical peak of nearly 130 percent in 1946, at the
end of World War II. Then as now, the government had spent the equivalent of trillions of dollars. However, the money spent in the 1940s was
used to create a solid foundation for growth. The United States emerged
from the war with the highest industrial capacity of any developed nation.
Our exports surged because we could supply in abundance products the
world needed. In turn, new industries provided a high number of well-
paying, middle-class jobs. The standard of living for both rich and poor
Americans soared. Economic growth took off and remained strong into
the 1960s and beyond.

Clearly, we need another such foundation, and building one would be
well worth the added debt. You see, one of the great things about strong
economic growth is that it makes debt more manageable. This is true
for individuals and nations alike. If you have large debts, you have only a
few options. You can consolidate your various loans to get a better interest rate, or you can reduce your spending, which is psychologically hard.

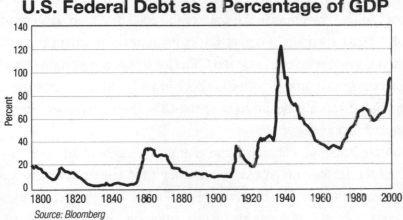

U.S. Federal Debt as a Percentage of GDP

Source: Bloomberg

But the absolute best way to make debt manageable is to increase your income. In fact, you could say the burden of debt is relative not primarily to income but to income growth. Hence borrowing money for education that leads to a better job is a good investment.

Similarly, everyone understands that businesses benefit when they take on debt in order to expand. "Good debt" is an investment that leads to higher revenues.

The problem in America today is that no one in government or out, on the left or the right, makes the distinction between bad government debt and good government debt—between spending and investment. They assume all debt is bad, which is not the case. The 2009 stimulus package was bad not because it increased debt but because it did not create investment in new growth industries.

Note that in advocating government investment, we are not promoting socialism. Capitalism often benefits directly from government investment. Such was the case with the industrialization program in World War II or the creation of the interstate highway system. Both programs increased productivity and corporate profits as well as median incomes. The key is for big government to be productive, not merely a tool of special interests. If we invest wisely, we have a chance to at least limit the damage the serious lack of vital resources will wreak on our economy.

Consider, too, the government investment that was the stimulus program launched by China in the wake of the 2008 recession. Relative to its GDP, China's spending program was many times larger than that of the United States. Yet no one criticized China for runaway government spending, because this program was all about investing in new industries and new jobs. It was a program to raise the GDP, thereby strengthening the country's financial state.

Committing our country to the energy equivalent of an Apollo space program to tackle the problems stemming from resource scarcity won't be enough, though. The opening shots of a war have been fired against America and we have to put the entire nation on a wartime footing if we are to avoid defeat. The costs of this war will ultimately far exceed those of any we've fought before—far more than the cold war, far more than World War II. Our failure to commit wholeheartedly to this war before it's too late will irreparably damage the future of Americans alive today and of all those yet to be born. The problem is, China already knows this and has built a tremendous head start in anticipation.

The difference between the two countries' nuclear power programs is but one example of this. In the United States, government loans for the construction of the first two new nuclear power plants in more than thirty years was greeted with great fanfare in 2010. China, meanwhile, has *more than thirty new nuclear plants* under construction, with many more units planned in the next three years alone.

The catastrophic accident at the Fukushima Daiichi Nuclear Power Station makes our resource situation all the more dire. As happened in the aftermath of the Three Mile Island accident (which, we must point out, resulted in no deaths), the tragic event in Japan is likely to set back the development of nuclear power in the United States and other Western countries by years, if not decades. China, on the other hand, will learn lessons from the Fukushima calamity but will proceed with the construction of nuclear reactors with great zeal.

Bear in mind that unlike at Fukushima, reactors built today incorporate third-generation nuclear technology, which have much higher pressure tolerances and can cool more easily, greatly reducing the risk of a repetition of the Japanese disaster. Local opposition to the development of nuclear power in the United States will likely ignore such arguments, however, as they seek a freeze on reactor construction. China's government, on the other hand, will not have to contend with an organized opposition, and the need for the reliable delivery of indispensible energy will trump safety concerns.

The United States garners less than 7 percent of its total energy consumed from alternative sources, and most of that comes from nuclear power. Our reliance on wind and solar barely moves the needle. We also lack ambitious goals for the rollout of alternative energy in the coming decade and beyond. The U.S. Energy Information Agency currently estimates that by 2035, renewable energy (including nuclear) will account for just 10.7 percent of our total energy usage, far less than China's stated goal for just the next ten years.

A prime example of China's commitment to alternative energy, which we would be wise to follow, is what they call the 863 Program (so named because it was first outlined in March 1986). Akin to ARPA-E, the U.S. Energy Department's Advanced Research Projects Agency—Energy, the 863 Program funnels government money into the research and development of a wide array of science and technology projects deemed strategic to China's economic and national security interests. Since 2001, the primary thrust of the 863 Program has been on alternative energy.

Funds from 863 have transformed China's wind power industry from essentially zero to the world leader in the last decade. The same can be said for solar power and coal gasification, to name just two other technologies. While the Obama administration funded ARPA-E with a paltry $400 million budget in 2009, the Chinese committed close to *$80 billion* (1.6 percent of their GDP) for high-tech development, with the lion's share allocated to alternative energy research.

Such a commitment on the part of America would not only be a good first step to put us on the road to greater energy security, but would prove to be an excellent engine for job creation—well-paying jobs that would bolster our economy. But more than that is needed: America's interests can no longer take a backseat to personal, corporate, or political interests.

Andrew Grove, the former chief of Intel, in a July 1, 2010, *Business-Week* editorial succinctly summed up a problem that has vexed our country: "Each company, ruggedly individualistic, does its best to expand efficiently and improve its own profitability. However, our pursuit of our individual businesses, which often involves transferring manufacturing and a great deal of engineering out of the country, has hindered our ability to bring innovations to scale at home. Without scaling, we don't just lose jobs—we lose our hold on new technologies. Losing the ability to scale will ultimately damage our capacity to innovate."

If the U.S. economy is to have a bright future we need to invest right away in new industries that address our most pressing problem of resource scarcity. And we can't allow the jobs that result from this investment to be offshored to foreign countries where land and labor costs are lower. As we've seen repeatedly during the past thirty years with China, the consequence would essentially be a gift to China with little benefit to ourselves. Yet despite this urgency, our leaders seem willing to offer only token agreement on the importance of these ideas.

There is no single silver bullet we can turn to for a solution to our predicament; it will require that we draw from every possible source at our disposal to rise to the challenge. And if, in the process, an important new technology is discovered, we need to keep it for ourselves—at least until we are sure that we won't surrender it to the Chinese or others before it is fully developed in the United States.

Earlier we discussed the Nobel Prize given to the two physicists who discovered graphene in 2004 as one possible answer. You'll recall that graphene has some unique properties that could lead to new ways to store and produce energy. It could lead to better integrated circuits, wind turbines, and solar cells that could help reduce our dependence on Middle East oil.

Sure, it will take many billions of dollars to develop graphene-based applications. But along with high-temperature superconducting, graphene may offer important solutions to the problems of energy scarcity. Its development should be of the highest priority, yet most people aren't even aware of its existence. It's so far from the public consciousness that the most up-to-date spell checkers on personal computers don't recognize graphene as a word—though they identify the names of many other things far less important or vital to our future. Clearly, our society has its priorities out of whack.

A Happier Ending?

Absent a dramatic drop in consumption throughout the world, resource scarcity points to a very dangerous and tumultuous future for all of humanity. And in this area, too, China appears to get it. For example, we have read a number of editorial pieces in the *Shanghai Daily* and other Chinese newspapers extolling the simple virtues of life and decrying consumption simply for the sake of consumption. At first these kinds of expostulations seem contradictory in a culture that is trying to encourage consumption. But they are not if you believe that there are natural boundaries to how high consumption can go.

Another question, which really gets to the heart of capitalism, is whether consumption for the sake of consumption is a worthy goal even without resource constraints. Most of us in America grew up with economists who preached that the acquisition of worldly things and well-being were one and the same. Most of economics is premised on this assumption. But lately—just in the past decade or so—perhaps as the result of the growing awareness of resource constraints or environmental issues, some economists have now begun to question the equation between happiness and material well-being.

One attempt to quantify both the benefits and the costs of a nation's economy activity is known as the genuine progress indicator (GPI), which factors quality-of-life indicators into the equation. Developed by social scientists Clifford Cobb, Ted Halstead, and Jonathan Rowe at the public policy institute Redefining Progress, GPI makes adjustments for income inequality between the rich and poor, adds the value of activities not included in GDP such as housework, parenting, and volunteer work, and subtracts for items such as the cost of lost leisure time, crime, and environmental degradation.

In contrast to nominal GDP, the GPI of the United States has declined markedly since the mid-1970s. In other words, our real wealth has deteriorated even as our financial wealth has increased, giving us a false sense of our well-being.

Genuine Progress Indicator

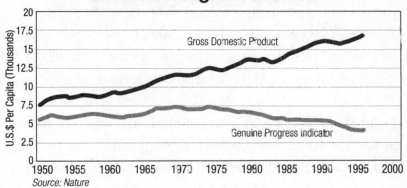

Source: Nature

Drawing from a similar playbook, Peter Victor, an economist at York University in Toronto and author of *Managing Without Growth: Slower by Design, Not Disaster*, has argued for a steady-state economy, in which we harness resources at a sustainable rate by slowing our growth for growth's sake and adopting objectives that enhance society's well-being. Victor acknowledges the challenges of such a dramatic change in our mindset, yet contends that not only can capitalism survive such a transition, but even in a shrinking economy some sectors, such as renewable energy development, will thrive. Still other economists, primarily in Europe, have argued for "degrowth": shrinking the developed world's economies to bring them into balance with environmental limits, while improving the quality of life. While this group is decidedly in the minority today, it is a movement that is likely to gain credibility going forward, either voluntarily or forcibly as materials scarcity and rising prices take a toll on consumers' wallets, prompting changes in their lifestyles.

In 2010, a wonderful summary of the idea of decoupling happiness and material well-being was published by the social economist Carol Graham in a book entitled *Happiness Around the World: The Paradox of Happy Peasants and Miserable Millionaires*. The book received a glowing review in the journal *Science*. In simple terms, as its subtitle indicates, the book summarizes a large number of studies that show happiness is not all about money. One study cited by Graham, for instance, shows that Nigerians are happier than the populations of many developed countries.

The book offers grounds for hope—hope that the world's plight does not have to end in resource wars, but perhaps in a less material but happier interrelated world society. In the last chapter Graham notes the following:

> Understanding what makes people happy and why may help us understand some of the fundamental questions in economics. What is the relationship between happiness and income? Happiness and health. . . . In fact, what makes people happy seems to be remarkably similar in all sorts of countries and contexts, from war-torn Afghanistan to new democracies like Chile and established ones like the United Kingdom. Increasing levels of income—and income growth—tend to be accompanied by rising expectations and related frustrations (at the macro level, the paradox of unhappy growth, and at the micro level, our frustrated achievers), across a surprisingly wide range of countries at different economic development levels. At the same time, we also found that individuals across the globe were remarkably adept at adapting expectations downwards when necessary. . . . Surely deep deprivation makes people unhappy, while many things that accompany higher levels of development, such as better public goods and less disease, make people happier.

The conclusions to Graham's book and the others mentioned above do indeed offer hope, especially when you consider that less resource consumption might lead to less disease and healthier lifestyles. The most hopeful sign is that achieving greater happiness does not require continued gains in income or material goods. To be sure, if that is the goal of capitalism, it is at variance with the underlying psychologies of much of the world's population, including that of America.

Leading the world into a regime where consumption for the sake of consumption is no longer the goal is not something any one country can accomplish alone. No doubt it will have to be led by the leader of the developed world and the leading nation in the developing world—America and China.

To say the least, the odds are not favorable. China is an insular society that does not trust the outside world—its major goal is a better life for its populace. Though there are already signs that the government recognizes that its populace will never be able to reach the level of material consumption that exists in America, it is still a far cry to say they would be willing to sit down with America and work out a resource-sharing scheme in time to avoid the conflict that ever more limited resources will involve.

For America it will be just as difficult to come to terms with the necessity of engaging China and agreeing to accept a lower standard of living. China, for one thing, is not a democracy and will be immediately suspect in any negotiations. If you permit us a speculation, possibly China could promise to transition to a democracy as an endpoint of the negotiations. But let's stop dreaming. Anything we say at this point other than the obvious necessity of engaging as quickly as possible with the Chinese and preparing for a lower living standard is utter guesswork.

If we fail, then it is much more likely to be more harmful to us than to the Chinese. Meaning it is much more likely that China will be able to stay together with what they have than it will be for America. Keep in mind that since 1952, China has survived two hideous drops in its economy. The first, in 1960–62 following on the heels of the "Great Leap Forward," saw its economy tumble by over 30 percent—closely matching our Depression. Several years of strong growth then gave way to another stunning loss in output during the "Cultural Revolution." Yet even with those drops China's annualized growth in real terms since 1952 has been over 7.5 percent. Little or no growth won't be easy to navigate even for China, but it will be easier for them than for America.

Not only do we have much farther to fall, but we also have far fewer resources to cushion the drop or to equally define a new standard of living. One hope is that our decline might be very slow, which might help. As Graham argues, countries can adjust to falling incomes and expectations, and to some extent the last decade or so proves the point. As we noted in our introduction, median household income in the United States dropped by about 10 percent during the period. Expectations may already be shifting. Recent surveys do not show a bubbly population that expects material well-being to continue to march upward. Instead, they indicate that we are preparing for further losses in our standard of living, and to some extent we have begun to accept that the good times are gone for good. Thus, America may be able to live with a slow fall, but we doubt that a sudden and massive drop in incomes would be easily accepted.

But just as Graham's summary of happiness research offers hope, histories of past civilizations leave no doubt about the obstacles we will confront. A book authored by David Wengrow in 2010, *What Makes Civilization? The Ancient Near East and the Future of the West*, strongly argues that the meshing of civilizations is not the natural course of human society. He notes that the history of the Near East shows "the deep attachment of human societies to the concepts they live by, and the inequalities they are prepared to endure in order to preserve those guiding principles." A reviewer of the book, Andrew Robinson, writing in *Nature*, notes, "This finding does not bode well for the current wars in Iraq and Afghanistan." Nor does it imply that a major rapprochement between China and America, not to mention the hundreds of other countries that share this planet, will be an easy task. But we have no choice. We have to try.

Index

Page numbers of charts and graphs appear in italics.

About the Authors

Dr. Stephen Leeb is a prolific author of books that present his macro-perspectives on global economic trends along with advice to investors. His books have been notable for predicting the secular bull market that began in the 1980s (*Getting in on the Ground Floor*, Putnam, 1986); the crash in tech stocks and the rise of real assets including oil and gold (*Defying the Market: Profiting in the Turbulent Post-Technology Market Boom*, McGraw-Hill, 1999); and the surge in oil prices (*The Oil Factor: Protect Yourself and Profit from the Coming Energy Crisis*, Warner Books, 2004). *Game Over: How You Can Prosper in a Shattered Economy* (Business Plus, 2009) predicted a permanent peak in global commodity production.

Dr. Leeb is founder, chairman, and chief investment officer of the Leeb Group, which publishes an extensive line of financial letters reaching more than 200,000 readers. The publications, which have received multiple awards for editorial excellence, include *The Complete Investor*, *Leeb's Income Performance Letter*, and *Leeb's Real World Investing*.

Further, as chairman and chief investment officer of Leeb Capital Management, a registered investment advisor, Dr. Leeb has been managing large-cap growth stock portfolios since 1999. Over the last decade, his portfolio has ranked among the best in its peer group, according to Informa's PSN manager database.

Dr. Leeb sits on various corporate boards, where he shares his strategic perspectives on financial markets and natural resources. Since 2008, Dr. Leeb has been a director of Plain Sight Systems, a Yale University–based technology holding company that owns a world-class patent portfolio in areas such as information organization/search, computational analytics, electro-optics, and spectroscopy. These technologies are critical in translating massive amounts of data into information and have applications across a multitude of major industries ranging from health care to cyber security to defense to financial analysis. He is a board member of Deep Markets Corporation, a division of Plain Sight Systems that is developing next-generation risk management applications.

Since 2006, Dr. Leeb has been head of the advisory board of Leor Exploration & Production LLC, a Houston-based oil and gas exploration company. Since 2007 he has served as a member of the advisory board of Electrum USA Ltd., one of the world's largest privately held gold exploration companies. He is also on the advisory board of Los Gatos, perhaps the world's largest privately held silver exploration company. Dr. Leeb also sits on the board of Water Intelligence plc, a publicly traded London-based company that has developed cutting-edge technology for managing water supplies.

Dr. Leeb earned his bachelor's degree in economics from the University of Pennsylvania's Wharton School of Business. In the following three years he obtained both a master's degree in mathematics and a Ph.D. in psychology from the University of Illinois.

GREGORY DORSEY has spent twenty-plus years as a portfolio manager, equities analyst, and stock market commentator. He joined the Leeb Group in 2004, and currently serves in the capacity of portfolio manager and member of the Investment Committee. His focus includes the natural resources sector, small-capitalization stocks, and income investments. In addition to his duties at Leeb Capital, Mr. Dorsey currently serves as editor for several Leeb Group publications.

Prior to joining the Leeb Capital Management team, Gregory ran an investment management firm, offering clients customized, tax-efficient portfolio management services.

Earlier in his career, Mr. Dorsey spent more than a decade as a newsletter editor at one of the nation's leading investment publishers. There, he researched stocks and provided readers with in-depth analysis of undervalued small stocks and general investment advice. In the process, he became adept at boiling down complex, often arcane issues into concise, easy-to-understand language, a rarity on Wall Street these days.

Mr. Dorsey has been widely quoted in the press and has provided his views on the stock market and the economy as a guest on many television and radio programs and at investment conferences around the country.

Mr. Dorsey holds a B.A. in economics and international relations from the University of Delaware.

**BUSINESS
PLUS**

Recognized as one of the world's most prestigious business imprints, Business Plus specializes in publishing books that are on the cutting edge. Like you, to be successful we always strive to be ahead of the curve.

Business Plus titles encompass a wide range of books and interests—including important business management works, state-of-the-art personal financial advice, noteworthy narrative accounts, the latest in sales and marketing advice, individualized career guidance, and autobiographies of the key business leaders of our time.

Our philosophy is that business is truly global in every way, and that today's business reader is looking for books that are both entertaining and educational. To find out more about what we're publishing, please check out the Business Plus blog at:

www.businessplusblog.com